Friendship, Cliques, and Gangs

Young Black Men Coming of Age in Urban America

D0963489

Friendship, Cliques, and Gangs

Young Black Men Coming of Age in Urban America

GREG DIMITRIADIS

Teachers College
Columbia University
New York and London

Published by Teachers College Press, 1234 Amsterdam Avenue, New York, NY 10027

Library of Congress Cataloging-in-Publication Data

Dimitriadis, Greg, 1969–
    Friendship, cliques, and gangs : young black men coming of age in urban America / Greg Dimitriadis.
      p. cm.
    Includes bibliographical references and index.
    ISBN 0-8077-4386-0 (cloth : alk. paper) — ISBN 0-8077-4385-2 (pbk. : alk. paper)
      1. African American youth. 2. African American youth—Social conditions.
    I. Title
    HQ797.D548   2003
    305.235—dc21   2003050759

ISBN 0-8077-4385-2 (paper)
ISBN 0-8077-4386-0 (cloth)

Printed on acid-free paper
Manufactured in the United States of America

10 09 08 07 06 05 04 03   8 7 6 5 4 3 2 1

We would like to dedicate this book, in loving memory, to Gloria, Shanika, Michael, and Andrew.

Contents

Acknowledgments

The first and most important debt I owe in writing this book is to the two young men I call Rufus and Tony. It was and is a profound privilege to be part of their lives. If nothing else, this book is a testament to our evolving relationship over (now) the past 6 years. I thank, as well, the young people and staff at the community center where this work began. In particular, I owe an incalculable debt to the unit director whom I call Johnny. This book, also, is a testament to his role in all three of our lives. It is painful to have to follow academic conventions and use pseudonyms for each. You're like family.

I would like to thank my colleagues and teachers at the University of Illinois. George Kamberelis (now of the University at Albany) was there for me in every way from the beginning and has been there every step of the way ever since. Thanks! My frequent coauthor Cameron McCarthy continues to spark my imagination and continues to inspire me with his expansive intellectual and pedagogical vision. I also thank Norman Denzin for his absolutely unwavering personal and professional support and for always making me feel as if I'm part of something much larger. Finally, my friends and fellow alumni Steven Bailey and Jonathan Sterne each read full drafts of this book and provided me with critical feedback and support. Thanks to you both.

I thank all my students and colleagues in the Graduate School of Education, the Department of Educational Leadership and Policy, and the Baldy Center for Law and Social Policy at the University at Buffalo for the wonderfully supportive environment. I thank, as well, Catherine

Cornbleth and Lois Weis for reading and commenting on early chapter drafts of this book. In particular, Lois read several chapters and finally a full draft of this book, providing critical feedback. As should be evident from this book, I also drew on her research and work in many different ways. It provided me with much of the courage to write this book.

I have many wonderful colleagues from around the country, way too numerous to mention. But they certainly include Dennis Carlson (with whom I have begun a very rewarding series of collaborations), Nadine Dolby (whose support and encouragement has been unwavering), Michael Apple, as well as Warren Crichlow. It also includes all of the scholars associated with the Bergamo conference and *JCT: Journal of Curriculum Theorizing*. This includes Bill Pinar, Marla Morris, John Weaver, and Peter Applebaum. Thank you all for the support and the inspiration.

Next, I would like to thank the staff at Teachers College Press. In particular, I would like to thank associate editor Catherine Bernard. Catherine had an unwavering faith in this project from the beginning, shepherding the proposal over and through some early rough moments. She provided constant feedback, helping to shape the writing and focus in critical ways. Catherine is truly an editor in the most classic sense of the term. I, quite literally, could not have done it without her. Thank you!

Finally, I would like to thank my entire family—in particular, my mother, father, and sister—for absolutely everything and then some.

A NOTE TO THE READER

In the interests of readability, I have edited some of the transcribed dialogue (e.g., pairing down the use of words and phrases such as "like" and "you know what I'm saying"), although I have not edited out what might be perceived as non-dominant grammar and word use. When I've removed words, I've generally used ellipses. I have also reconstructed some dialogue from extended and (I believe) meticulous field notes. Finally, as noted above, names of people and places and some details that could identify participants have been changed throughout. Of course, I take full responsibility for all such decisions.

CHAPTER ONE

Engaging the Complex Lives of Contemporary Youth

That life is complicated may seem a banal expression of the obvious, but it is nonetheless a profound theoretical statement—perhaps the most important theoretical statement of our time.
—Avery Gordon, *Ghostly Matters: Haunting and the Sociological Imagination*, p. 3

I think that all theories are suspect, that the finest principles may have to be modified, or may even be pulverized by the demands of life.
—James Baldwin, "Autobiographical Notes," p. 9

In many ways, this story both begins and ends late in October of 1998, in the intensive care unit of a hospital in a small Midwestern city I call "Hub City." Rufus, 17, had just brought his mother, Mary, in for treatment. She had gained 30 pounds in one month and had complained to her doctor that the weight gain was not normal, that somehow, as she told the doctor, "this isn't me." The doctor, however, assumed it was due to her not following her careful diet (which she wasn't) and told her to leave his office. The doctor's tough love tactics aside, it turned out that the weight gain was due to kidney failure. Her diabetes had eaten away at her kidneys and her body, quite literally, had filled up with waste.

Like many poor people, Mary only visited the hospital when she reached a critical stage, which was where she was now. She would be in the hospital for a week and would soon go back home, though she would return a month later to this same hospital under even more dire circumstances. Rufus was with her here, now as always, missing yet another day of school. There was no other option. As both pointed out to me time and again, they had to rely on each other for everything—emotional as well as material support. But Rufus also served a more practical purpose here that day. Mary did not always quite get everything the doctors said and Rufus was able to explain things to her in a way she could understand. Mary told me several times that she needed someone to help her talk to the doctors—her son or maybe a neighbor. It could even be me—"a close friend of the family," as she put it. But in the end it was usually, such exceptions aside, Rufus.

Rufus and Mary had spent a lot of time together at this hospital and would spend even more over the next several months. The days and nights were typically uneventful—chatting with the guards and the nurses, playing "spades" (if he came with friends and someone had cards), seeing if anyone had left snacks behind in the waiting room, and so forth. But today, Rufus heard something more exciting—commotion from out in the hallway. Someone was yelling, "Get off me! Get off me! Get off me!" As Rufus walked out the door, he heard his mom yell, "Mind your business, boy!" Here, in the hallway, he saw orderlies trying to restrain Tony, 18, who was fighting them violently. Tony's head was bandaged— he had suffered what looked like a very bad, very serious head wound. In fact, one of Tony's friends had become hysterical at the park when he saw the blood because it was so thick and shiny, the wound so clearly devastating. Tony would not remember being hit with the bat, nor being taken to the hospital, nor fighting everyone every step of the way, nor having to be physically restrained. Longer stretches of memory would be lost forever. For restraining him, the hospital added $40 onto the already $600+ charge for the ambulance. A week later, when Tony returned from the hospital, he would joke that he got upset when they gave him the bill. On a more serious note, he complained that if he was well enough to fight the orderlies, attendants, and doctors, he was well enough to get himself to the hospital and somehow, he should not have to pay the bill. In fact, he had gone into shock.

When Rufus saw Tony, he told the doctors immediately, "That's my brother!" The doctors were relieved that someone so close to him was there, and soon, with Rufus's strong, helpful presence, Tony was in a hospital room, his head literally stapled together, a battery of neurological tests underway. The incident would be a small blurb in the local paper— man gets beaten—though the paper would link the incident to gang rivalries and note that the police around the park where it happened were on alert for possible gang-like retaliation. However, the truth, as always, was more complex.

The conflict began several days earlier. One of Tony's close friends, Willie, overheard another young person, Chris, talking about another of Tony and Willie's friends, Cortez. This was reported back to Cortez, who confronted Chris, who in turn denied it. All were ostensibly members of the same gang, though each claimed that the other was not "true" or fully initiated. Threats went back and forth—typically through indirect channels—for several days. The fight culminated in a local park, where Tony, a member of the same gang, accompanied Cortez. Cortez and Chris were finally going to fight it out, one-on-one, man to man. As Tony said later on the local news, he wanted to make sure that his friend had a fair fight. For whatever reason, Tony's presence was threatening to those there with Chris. The last thing Tony remembered hearing was someone yelling, "Get him! Get him!" Chris's friend Charles then hit Tony in the back of the head with an aluminum bat. Several weeks later, Chris's brother Akmed, a member of a rival gang, would send Tony (along with another cousin) back to the hospital for giving his brother's name to the police.

The meeting between Rufus and Tony in the hospital was, on one level, pure coincidence. What were the chances that the two would almost literally bump into each other under such circumstances? Later on, Rufus would try to explain away the incident by saying that he had had a "bad feeling" that day, like something like this might happen. It would be too prescient for me to say that I had a similar "bad feeling," though in retrospect, the meeting seemed almost bound to happen—each of their ways of engaging with the world, their "survival strategies" as I came to call them, taken to their logical conclusions. Tony, always putting himself on the line, always in search of respect, nearly beaten to death. Rufus, always in the background, always supportive of others, acting as primary caretaker for his mom. Their meeting in the hospital, under these circumstances, seemed near-destined to happen, the stark and seemingly apparent differences in their lives underscoring their perhaps peculiar friendship once again.

Indeed, in the popular imagination about young black men, Rufus and Tony had followed the only two available paths—one (Rufus) was "good" while the other (Tony) was "bad." Though I had heard each refer to the other as, alternatively, "cousin" and "brother" over the several years I had known them, they were in fact best friends. Tony and Rufus's story made up part of my book *Performing Identity/Performing Culture: Hip Hop as Text, Pedagogy, and Lived Practice,* a long-term ethnography of young people and their uses of hip hop at a local community center in the urban Midwest. It consisted of historical and theoretical commentary as well as three extended ethnographic case studies. I argued in this book that reception practices—how young people picked up and responded to these hip hop texts—were unpredictable and became more so when moving from local social networks to individual biographies.

I wrote this book, in part, to contest the ways hip hop culture and music have come to index the so-called nihilism of contemporary black youth. It was, in many respects, a neatly contained, celebratory story (though I could not have articulated this at the time). In fact, late in 1998, as I visited Rufus's mother and Tony in near adjacent hospital rooms, I was deep in the writing process, ever-sharpening and honing their story for public presentation and publication. Facing personal and professional deadlines, I was at the writing stage of my ethnographic endeavors, which demanded I give clear shape and form to amorphous experiences, and demanded that I "liberate events from the untidiness of everyday life so that they can be 'read' like articles, books, or, as we now say, *texts*" (Rosaldo, 1993, p. 12). I was, in large measure, writing up a neat story about the "past," teasing out implications for the "future," just as the "present" was unraveling in front of me.

In this less tidy real world, Tony lay in a hospital bed with life-threatening head trauma while Rufus sat alone by his mother's side as she began a long road to an early death. In this world, I could no longer assume the role, privilege, or importance of popular culture. Here, my ability to distance myself from the particulars of their everyday lives, to bring narrative closure to their lives, was challenged at every turn. Here, "the everyday" could be fundamentally rearticulated very quickly in ways that could overwhelm and overshadow my work and my life. Indeed, Tony would soon get better, only to be attacked by Chris's brother. He would leave town under threat, and go to the same southern hometown he and Rufus romanticized in their daily lives and talk. Rufus would also return to the South but it would be to bury his mother, who died 9 months later, after an extended stay in the hospital and in a nursing home. The reunion down South—which I attended, as well—would mark one of the few times they spent together since that day in the hospital.

Friendship, Cliques, and Gangs: Young Black Men Coming of Age in Urban America is my effort to tell a different, more complex and personal kind of story about these extraordinary youth. Rufus and Tony, as I will show, challenged stereotypes and assumptions about "good" verses "bad" youth, while they tried to meet multiple kinds of demands, in ways that always exceeded my ready-made interpretive frameworks. Each, I came to see, had to struggle individually and together by drawing on a range of resources—local institutions, key older figures, and friends—in navigating their own largely improvised pathways out of adolescence. Over the years I knew them, *struggle*—in all its various permutations and particularities—emerged as the one and only constant in their lives.

Experiencing these immediacies as researcher, club staff member, and eventually (I like to believe) trusted friend forced me to ask different kinds of questions about young people, the dangers and challenges they face, the survival strategies they develop, and the ways they make sense out of it all. A different agenda emerged with time, and in retrospect, one I will pursue in this book. More specifically, I argue here that understanding Rufus and Tony's lives will go a long way towards helping us challenge dominant ideas about "normal" or "successful" adolescent development and the ways they inform increasingly popular and prevalent notions of urban youth and how we serve them. Revisiting these notions of adolescence and urban youth will allow us, I hope, to "remap" pedagogical possibilities with and for young people today—possibilities that look beyond the often constraining institutional pathways we as educators, researchers, and policy makers have laid out for them (Dimitriadis & Weis, 2001). Indeed, if ideas about "normal" development have buttressed dominant ideas about "proper" schooling (as I will make clear shortly), then alternative notions of adolescence might inform a different—and perhaps more progressive and expansive—agenda for education today.

TRADITIONAL VIEWS OF ADOLESCENCE AND "AT-RISK" YOUTH

Traditionally, social psychologists have described "adolescence" as an "in-between" stage between childhood and adulthood, a time when young people struggle to define themselves by trying different identities on and off. This notion of adolescence, as Wyn and White (1997) point out, "assumes a 'pre-social' self . . . which exists within the individual but which must be found and developed ('finding one's self'). The individual is seen as distinct from and separate from society, as possessing a 'self' independent from social relationships or social circumstances" (p. 53). With this logic, moving from adolescence to adulthood means moving from a state of dependency to one of independence and autonomy. In particular, reaching adulthood means separating one's self (materially and otherwise) from one's family and parents. Burton, Obeidallah, and Allison sum up,

> Adolescence in contemporary American society is traditionally defined as a transition period, marking the change from childhood to adulthood. Occurring between the ages of eleven to twenty, normative adolescent development is characterized by qualitative biological, social, and cognitive changes for the individual. . . At the social level, adolescence is characterized as a life period when individuals develop increasing autonomy with respect to their relationships with their parents and family. (1996, p. 397)

Developing such relative autonomy, however, is a struggle and young people face multiple dangers in this transition. Indeed, this discourse of adolescence and development is intimately tied to the very familiar discourse of "at-risk" youth. For example, Joy Dryfoos's recent book, *Safe Passage: Making it through Adolescence in a Risky Society*, argues that youth must navigate their way past the multiple dangers (drugs, gangs, unwanted pregnancy, etc.) that impede a "safe passage" to adulthood. Young people are positioned here (albeit reflectively) "as vulnerable [at risk] because a number of influences may occur which irreparably damage the process of growing up as 'normal'" (p. 54). This discourse on at-risk youth is largely a normative one, one that reinforces fairly stable a priori notions of adolescence and adulthood and the "proper" transition from one to the other.

Though still very much a part of the popular imagination about youth, these notions about adolescent development and autonomy have recently been called into question by a range of theorists and researchers who have looked more closely at question of "social context." For example, in his book *Adolescents and their Families*, Stuart Hauser discusses how young people's families can "promote new patterns of individual autonomy" and also, quite importantly, experience "connectedness with others" (1991, p. 5). While Hauser is very much invested in normative notions of adolescent development, he highlights the role of "connectedness" in the transition out of adolescence and into adulthood—not only "autonomy." He sums up, "This daunting combination of social and biological forces generates the deep challenge and paradox of adolescent development: to separate from the family while connecting with it in new ways" (p. 3).

Others such as Lawrence Steinberg have extended and developed this discussion of the social aspects of adolescent development in important ways. Indeed, in a series of influential commentaries, Steinberg (1996a; 1996b) argues that we must explore the social contexts of development in all their complexity, both locally and more broadly. This includes exploring how developmental pathways are "socially influenced by others in the adolescent's proximal environment," including family and peer groups. It also means understanding how development is "contextually limited by the broader ecology" of young people's worlds (1996a, p. 253). If nothing else, Steinberg socially situates the process of development, thus calling into question broad-brushed, a priori notions of "proper" adolescent development.

These academic interventions have been critical for helping us rethink traditional notions of adolescent development. However, it is important to note that these more traditional normative assumptions about adolescence have had an enormous durability in the popular imagination. For example, such assumptions have largely buttressed contemporary notions about schooling both in theory and in practice (Dryfoos, 1998). Under this logic, young people are presumed to move incrementally through stages—from elementary school to middle school to high school to college—under the tutelage and varied assistance of more skilled adults. Young people are typically presumed to need heavy "scaffolding" early on, but are expected to develop more and more intellectual and personal autonomy along the way. Accordingly, those who do "poorly" in school are typically assumed to be "at risk" in one way or another, often spawning school reform efforts that try to "capture youth adrift" from what might be considered "normal" developmental expectations (Lesko, 2001, p. 94).

These notions of "at-risk" youth—notions that typically put social issues in the background in favor of psychological ones—have proven itself to be particularly ill-equipped to deal with the lives, experiences, and needs of disenfranchised, minority youth. Interestingly, the literature has been almost completely silent in this regard. As McLoyd and Steinberg (1998) write, "Although ethnicity has been a focus of concern for several decades among anthropologists and, to a lesser degree, sociologists, leading journals in adolescent development continue to show a conspicuous paucity of research in this area" (p. vii). This lack of research has obscured focus on a very specific set of issues and concerns vis-à-vis non-white and disenfranchised youth.

Indeed, for many such youth, adolescence is an ambiguous life stage with competing "role expectations" and mixed messages about "successful" development (Burton, Obeidallah, & Allison, 1995, p. 120). Middle-class norms about distinct life stages and clear transitions do not wholly apply here. Perhaps most importantly, everyday material demands often bring the worlds of parents and children together in ways that belie a neat separation between the two. For example, middle-class adolescents and adults have traditionally used income level and job status to mark generation distinctions. However, many marginalized youth work side by side with their parents in service sector "McJobs"—often the only available work for people without advanced degrees—and must contribute all or part of that income to household maintenance (p. 130). Poor black youth like Rufus and Tony often have the kinds of responsibilities—including financial ones—that preclude a so-called normal childhood. For these young people, increasingly stronger affective and material ties with family and community are often necessitated by everyday struggle. To echo the powerful work of Alex Kotlowitz (1992), "There are no children here." Clear lines and demarcations between those older and younger are typically blurred or simply nonexistent, raising a series of key problematics.

The case of schools is particularly telling. For many marginalized youth, what it takes to succeed at school often works at cross purposes with what it takes to succeed in their local communities. For example, one must often uncritically defer to authority in schools while having to assume tremendous amounts of authority outside of school. Burton, Obeidallah, and Allison (1996) write,

> Within the context of the school setting, adolescents are often treated like "older children" who require assisted learning. At home, however, some inner-city adolescents are treated like "grown folks," often saddled with adult responsibilities that are in direct conflict with the "older child" treatment and adult monitoring they receive in school. (p. 403)

They offer a poignant quote from one of their teenage participants in this regard: "Do this, do that. School says one thing. Momma says another. Am I a young man, grown man, or a child? You tell me" (p. 405).

This kind of "confusion" was borne out in my own work as well. Rufus, for example, had tremendous amounts of responsibility from a very young age, acting as brother, friend, confidant, son, and even father to Mary. He chided her into following her strict diet. He had to comfort her when the bills looked insurmountable. He had to control her like a child when she turned hysterical in the hospital, claiming that the doctors were trying to kill her. He also told me again and again that he, too, was a child and needed the support and guidance of those who were older. Tony, in turn, had to act as a father figure for his younger brother (Rick's biological dad was in jail), as well as bring necessary income into his household. I have heard him talk often while shopping about what "the kids"—meaning his younger brothers and sister—would want to eat. I have seen him check the nutritional value on products, then carefully check different prices, always getting generic if possible. I have seen him cash his minimum wage check to do this. I have also seen him get dragged—and sometimes drag others—into very serious gang-related conflicts that betrayed his adolescence, his need for local acceptance with teenage peers. It is hard, of course, to clearly demarcate developmental stages and boundaries here, making any sort of normative evaluation of their "life outcomes" difficult if not impossible.

Indeed, while theirs is in many respects a "success" story—in ways I will develop most clearly in the concluding chapter—it is perhaps an unlikely one. As Burton, Obeidallah, and Allison (1995) note, what counts as "successful" development is radically context-specific, as communities of youth and adults often have "alternative perspectives about what merit[s] a successful developmental outcome in their environment." These alternative perspectives reflect the various realities of survival in local communities and offer us new ways to think about developmental outcomes (p. 131). They offer an excellent example, quoting a community leader from their research, who comments upon a neighborhood teen named Anthony:

> Anthony may not have finished high school, he may not have a job, but he is the treasure of our community. He helps the young mothers around the neighborhood with their kids. He does the grocery shopping for some of the older folks around here who can't get out. And he keeps the peace between rival street gangs in the community. (1996, p. 402)

The challenge throughout this book will be to articulate another such story, another such perspective on what might count as a "successful" outcome. I hope and believe that these kind of stories, in all their particularity, will help counter the universalizing claims about urban youth so prevalent and influential today among educators, policy makers, and researchers alike.

In closing this brief section on adolescence and "at-risk" youth, I would like to highlight a recent discussion with Tony, a discussion that typifies many of the contradictions and complexities around what counts as "success" for these young men. The week had been tough for him. He called me collect. A few weeks earlier, Tony had been expelled for the second time from Job Corps for drinking. He had once again undermined his own desire to leave home and "make something" of himself—he had been studying to be a short-order cook. In addition, he had a run-in with the police just that afternoon. Tony had been driving with his cousin Jill in her brother Derrick's car, when the police pulled them over. Derrick had a warrant out for him and Jill had a suspended license. It had little to do with Tony. But, as in the past, Tony's temper flared and he wound up in a shouting match with the officers. The police detained his cousin and Tony had to walk the three or so miles back home. This was tiring and also dangerous. Charles, the teen who had hit him with the bat, was just out of jail after 2 years and he feared another conflict.

Finally, Tony's friend G-Boy had recently been sentenced to 30 years in jail for the armed robbery of a food delivery man. Due to be sentenced along with him was Tony's cousin Nicky. Nicky had, according to Tony, been in the wrong place at the wrong time. Tony was convinced that if he could have afforded a better lawyer, he would have been acquitted. He didn't have a gun, Tony said, and was just hanging out with G-Boy when it all happened. However, he was going to take a plea bargain that would force him to serve 15 years. The DA had threatened 30, according to Tony, and Nicky began weeping on the spot. Like nearly all of Tony's cousins, Nicky was on probation, which made all such infractions immeasurably more serious. So, he took what seemed the best option—half the jail time.

Nicky was the latest in the long line of Tony's cousins to be jailed. One by one, over the 6 or so years I knew them, nearly all seemed to disappear (for varying amounts of time) for offences minor and major—from drunk and disorderly conduct to selling drugs. Even Tony's younger brother Rick was in juvenile hall for curfew violation. Offering a comforting ear that evening, it struck me just how very extraordinary—or perhaps lucky—Tony was. Unemployed, without a high school diploma, nearly homeless, Tony had managed to avoid (for at least a time) perhaps the gravest danger facing his generation—incarceration. He was, at the same time, learning to control a temper that often got him into trouble, as well as a drinking problem that got him kicked out of Job Corps. These were serious problems for sure, especially when they fed off of each other. But he was working to control them—the temper that still, at times, got him in trouble with the law and the drinking problem that, at one point, led to a serious pancreas problem. He was also a success, volunteering at the local community center, struggling hard to be a good role model for his siblings, and looking to Rufus—his self-professed best friend and personal hero—for necessary support through it all.

REARTICULATING THE
RESEARCHER/RESEARCHED DIVIDE

In *Friendship, Cliques, and Gangs: Young Black Men Coming of Age in Urban America* I chart the various and particular struggles of these young men as I understood and experienced them over a 5-year period. Specifically, I highlight several different sets of resources Rufus and Tony drew upon for survival and support as they traveled through adolescence to early adulthood.

To begin with, I highlight the complex role of friendship in their daily lives. Young men like Rufus and Tony, as I demonstrate, are enmeshed in important, local friendship networks that are often invisible to—and misunderstood by—those older (Allan, 1998; Dimitriadis, 2001a). I also highlight the importance of the various unofficial educational institutions these teens traverse. Though largely ignored in literature on youth, alternative educational sites—for example, YMCAs, Boys & Girls Clubs, and churches—are doing much of the pedagogical work traditionally and ostensibly performed in schools, in ways I will explore and develop. Next, I highlight all the ways in which these teens draw on key older figures for relevant support and mentoring relationships. Young people like Rufus and Tony, as a number of contemporary scholars have made clear, are accessing a wider range of older models in unpredictable though critical ways. In sum, I highlight these three sets of resources as they are rooted in the lived realities of these teens, as they deepen our understanding of young people and their complex pathways from adolescence to adulthood.

I explore, finally, the ways I became another resource for support and survival, in ways that rearticulated my relationship with each as well as my identity as a white researcher "in the field." For Tony, providing this support meant trips to McDonald's or rides to the store or work or copies of rap CDs. After he was assaulted and nearly killed, it meant visits to the hospital with various goods or simple companionship when he was in fear of further retaliation from his rivals. For Rufus, who had only his mom, providing this support meant hauling large bags of clothes to the laundromat, cashing social security checks, and going grocery shopping at discount stores out of town. It also included, in the last months of his mother's life, constant trips back and forth with Rufus to the hospital, the nursing home, and the dialysis center. All of this helped me understand the importance and immediacies of day-to-day survival for these teens, challenging my initial research agenda as well as the boundaries between my "professional" and "personal" lives.

Friendship, Cliques, and Gangs is thus a very personal book for me. It can't be otherwise. As I will make clear throughout this book, ethnographers today no longer have recourse to notions of objectivity or distance from those we study. There are no safe or pure spaces from which to research and write. We inhabit different and often contradictory personal and political roles and expectations "in the field" and "at our desks," allowing for particular knowledges with specific effects. To echo Michelle Fine (1994), fieldworkers today must "work the hyphen" in these different roles and identities, always acknowledging the roles we inhabit, what they allow, and what they deny. As Fine notes, "By *working the hyphen*, I mean to suggest that researchers probe how we are in relation with the contexts we study and with our informants, understanding that we are all multiple in those relations" (p. 72). Fine joins a growing number of scholars and critics in asking us to look past the traditional researcher-subject binary split to new and different kinds of relationships with new and different kinds of possibilities.

I take this charge very seriously. As indicated above, I continually wrestled with this researcher-subject binary over the course of my work, in ways that allowed me to understand the lives of these teens in more open and less prefigured ways. Indeed, we are at a moment in time when a priori assumptions about young people and educative texts, institutions, and policies are open to renegotiation (Dimitriadis & Carlson, 2003; Dimitriadis & McCarthy, 2001). A willingness to "work the hyphen" between "self" and "other" is a basic starting point, I believe, for understanding and addressing the specific needs and concerns of contemporary youth.

THE CHAPTERS

I begin with a discussion of Rufus and Tony and their friendship network, rooted in place and in extended family from the South. As noted, Rufus and Tony have followed two very different life courses. While they called each other "cousin" and "brother," they were in fact the best of friends. Growing up as very young boys in the same small town in Mississippi, both made the trip to the Midwest about a decade earlier. While Tony had a large family here, including numerous aunts and, most especially, cousins, Rufus had only his mother. He referred, however, to all of Tony's cousins as his own. This group—Tony and Rufus and several of Tony's cousins—made up what they all called a "clique." I discuss the ways both

used this "clique" for both similar and different kinds of social and personal support. I discuss, as well, the differences between this clique and
several local gangs to which many in the clique also belonged. These networks are very much about the shifting nature of local needs and mean
very different things to different young people at different times. They are
critical and misunderstood resources in the lives of the young.

Next, in Chapter 3, I look at the importance of a local community
center in the lives of Tony and Rufus—how this site opened up unique,
validated pathways to success in their lives as well as how unexpected
events largely subverted this success. Both were members of this center
or "club" from a young age. Both became staff members when they got
older. In particular, I highlight the summer of 1997 when we all worked
together at this club. I describe how Tony and Rufus were able to embody
validated, authoritative roles in ways that proved transformative for them.
Though neither had much success in school, both decided to become
teachers when the summer ended. This decision was rooted in a profound
sense of care for young people at this site. As Tony said in August, "Nan
[not] one of them is bad." These institutions, I argue, thrive on the complex, already-existing social networks of young people—their ability to
bring specific sets of personal resources to bear on concrete concerns and
challenges. However, they are also subject to all the real-world events and
issues that are invited by the lives of marginalized youth. Indeed, while
Rufus and Tony took on more permanent staff positions beginning in the
fall of 1997, each had to leave due to complex, personal contingencies.
This tension, I argue, is a challenging paradox for educational researchers
and policy makers today.

In Chapter 4, I discuss how Rufus and Tony understood what it
meant to "grow up" and become validated authority figures for others.
My focus is twofold. First, I discuss their understanding of and relationship with a key older figure in their lives—Johnny, the unit director of the
community center. I show how their relationship with Johnny confound-
ed assertions about the loss of so-called old heads in urban communities
today. Johnny provided a distinct kind of model for what it meant to be a
validated and valued adult, to occupy an authority role in this neighborhood. Second, I discuss how these youth strove to become adults in the
context of their everyday lives and activities. In contrast with much of the
sociological work on old heads, I focus on the work of young people

themselves in this process of self-definition. Through a close look at several such activities, I show young people working to articulate their social networks in new, more positive directions, both looking to older people like Johnny for guidance while trying to be there for those younger.

In the concluding chapter, I come full circle and discuss how this volume can help us better understand urban youth and the complex challenges they face today. I stress the theme of *survival* which has implicitly permeated this book—how Tony and Rufus fought against overwhelming odds to carve out lives for themselves by drawing on a range of resources. Updated by current information, I discuss what both teens are doing today and what this tells us about how we define "successful outcomes." More locally grounded understandings of developmental paths to adulthood, I argue, can help us forge institutions and policies more in touch with the everyday concerns of marginalized youth. I pay special attention to other key and related institutions in their lives—in particular the legal and medial institutions that became so important to each. I conclude with some reflections on the changing nature of education today, as well as the need to rearticulate the researcher/researched divide.

FINAL THOUGHTS

To echo Avery Gordon, life is complicated. Perhaps now a cliché, this notion, evoked at the outset of this chapter, has taken on new meaning and significance for me throughout the process of researching and writing this book. No subject has challenged me as much as the lives of two "ordinary" young people. No writing project has so exceeded my ability to contain it. The "demands of life," as James Baldwin writes, again and again forced me to reevaluate, rearticulate, and rewrite. I recall here the disorienting days late in 1998 evoked at the outset of this chapter—as I spent many uncertain and frightening hours with Rufus and Tony in the hospital—as I simultaneously attempted to give their lives coherence and shape in my writing.

Ultimately, I try to tell a different kind of story about contemporary urban youth—one that challenges the ways in which they have been pathologized in the popular imagination while speaking as honestly as possible about their often brutal lives and everyday realities. Above all else, I try not to tell a simple story of "good" and "bad" youth, but of a relationship that transcends such distinctions, pointing to new and different ways to think about young people and the institutions that serve them. Telling such a story means abandoning any pretence to objectivity and emotional distance on my part. It means thinking of ethnography as a profoundly ethical, personal, and relational human practice. *Friendship, Cliques, and Gangs: Young Black Men Coming of Age in Urban America* is not the book I set out to write. It is a book that emerged from the complicated and unpredictable ground of our friendship, addressing questions I did not intend to ask and agendas I did not presume to dictate. It is a book, I hope, that will help begin a more complex and less arrogant conversation about urban youth—a conversation that does justice to their extraordinary lives, pressing needs, and critical concerns.

CHAPTER TWO

Friendship, Cliques, and Gangs: Social Support in the Lives of Young Black Men

We must rethink traditional notions of "success," I noted in the last chapter, if we are to do justice to the complex lives of young black men. In this chapter, I focus more clearly on the ways these young men worked to create and sustain unique kinds of friendships, modes of association and affiliation which helped them avoid the pitfalls of gang life. A close look at these kinds of relationships is important, I argue, if we are to move beyond simple ways of sorting, classifying, and labeling young men, if we are to move beyond reductive and debilitating notions of "good" versus "bad" youth, and the radical individuation these distinctions often imply.

BLACK MEN AND FRIENDSHIP

There is not much work on black men and friendship. The literature that exists tends to focus on black manhood as a radically individualizing experience, on associations between black men as violent and criminalized. For example, Richard Majors' and Janet Billson's influential *Cool Pose: The Dilemmas of Black Manhood in America* (1992) explored the coping strategies young black men use to deal with threatening social demands and pressures. They write:

Of all the strategies embraced by black males to cope with oppression and marginality, the creation of the cool pose is perhaps the most unique. Presenting to the world an emotionless, fearless, and aloof front counters the low sense of inner control, lack of inner strength, absence of stability, damaged pride, shattered confidence, and fragile social competence that come from living on the edge of society. (p. 8)

They continue, arguing that "tough talk and aggressive posturing are valid ways of expressing coolness" (p. 29). According to the authors, this leaves little room for nurturing relationships either between black men or between black men and women.

When we do see notions of community among black men, it is usually through the relatively large and methodologically diverse body of work on contemporary gangs (Bing, 1992; Cummings & Monti, 1993; Jankowski, 1991; Klein, 1995; Shakur, 1998). This work has tended to focus on gangs as modes of association for disenfranchised youth—modes of association linked to antisocial behavior. "Gangs," according to Jankowski (1991), "find themselves having to socialize a group of people who have certain attributes that are useful for a gang, but nearly all these individuals also possess certain qualities that are potentially divisive" (p. 86). These qualities are, in many respects, similar to the radically individuating pressures Major and Billson point out in *Cool Pose*. This is accomplished by fostering the attitude that "all the members of the gang [are] brothers . . . that if members could come to think of themselves as brothers, they would be likely to develop more respect for fellow members and ultimately more empathy for the gang as a whole" (p. 86). Discussions of "the brotherhood ideology," of course, permeate nearly all of this literature, with the very common and reductive notion that one's gang is one's "family." While this work has quite powerfully documented the bonds that draw these young men together, it is of course exclusively in an antisocial context. Missing is work that looks at these kinds of bonds in ways that transcend these often stereotypical confines.

Most of the work on social support has tended to focus on women. For example, Carol Stack's *All Our Kin* (1974) highlights the importance of supportive networks for dealing with poverty, noting especially the strategic work of women. In another key example, Ruth Sidel's *Urban Survival: The World of Working Class Women* (1978) focused on the narratives of varied working-class women as they detailed their day-to-day struggles. More recently, Michelle Fine and Lois Weis's *The Unknown City* (1998) has looked at the lives of poor and working-class young adults in the United States. Here, they show how African-American women "live in a line of women" and "hold together to raise the next generation, retaining connectedness through sharing resources and by many individually leaning on God in the midst of private and public assault" (pp. 184–185). In all these cases, the authors stress the caring and supportive bonds that women forge between each other.

Some recent work has tried to bring these concerns with social support to work on men. Perhaps most notably, Mitchell Dunier (1992) has contested the "cool pose" image of men as a debilitating stereotype, positing the lives of older black men in a Chicago neighborhood as an alternative to this radically individuating model. His book, *Slim's Table*, is an ethnography of a local diner, Valois, on the city's South Side. Indeed, when discussing an interaction between Leroy, an older black man, and Bart, an older, ailing white man, he notes:

> Though black men are usually portrayed as so consumed with maintaining a cool pose that they are unable to "let their guard down and show affection," these black men created a caring community in which one of the men, Leroy, has even expressed his feelings for Bart by telling him the men were interested in his illness because they loved him. (p. 20)

These men, according to Dunier, embodied deeply held values of respect for themselves and others, embodied in an ethic of mutual support and care.

These men, according to Dunier, offer models for manhood missing from extant sociological literature, books like *Soulside*, *Urban Blues*, and *Tally's Corner*. While these books have attempted to explore black neighborhoods, stressing their own cultural dynamics, they have tended to reinforce dominant ideas about black masculinity, with tales of physical and verbal aggression, hyper-masculinity, sexual conquest, and general distain for work. The men in Dunier's study, however, provide another kind of model and he does a wonderful job detailing the lives. Yet in many respects, Dunier uncritically echoes their stereotypes about younger black men—young men like Rufus and Tony. He writes,

> Their outlook toward the black population of the area is also commonly expressed in statements about younger, lower-class blacks. . . . Besides being criticized for their mode of dress, a general flashiness in demeanor,

and an inability to communicate, younger blacks are often accused of being unwilling to work. (p. 69)

As one man, Elvin, said, "It's sad. Every young kid in school has either got a weapon, or dope, or he's gonna rob you. If he wants his fix, he's gonna get you. It doesn't matter who you are. You can be his best friend" (p. 70).

Dunier thus looks towards the more caring modes of affiliation between black men, contesting the radically individuating modes that have marked books like *Cool Pose*. Quite laudably, he contests the ways black men have been represented in contemporary sociological and popular literature. However, Dunier remains largely silent on the lived realities of these youth. He rather unproblematically echoes many of the sentiments and concerns of older black men. This seems, to me, a serious elision, one that obscures the everyday lives of these young men—everyday realities that both reflect the kind of sociological literature that Dunier references and transcends it.

Slim's Table, in sum, starkly highlights and reinforces an all-too-familiar good/bad binary in its treatment of black youth. This binary, it is critical to note, is underscored in much contemporary literature. In one memorable recent account, *Hope in the Unseen* (1998), Ron Suskind details the life of one young teen—Cedric Jennings—on his way to an Ivy League college, and his efforts to resist the temptations of the streets. The "streets" remain nebulous and nefarious in this account, which constructs them as a homogenous "other" unsuccessfully holding back the protagonist as he makes his way to and through Brown University. In many respects, the book evidences the social isolation of Cedric, isolation from his peers, his neighborhood, as well as from other students at Brown. Early on the author notes, "Cedric Jennings is not, by nature, a loner, but he finds himself ever more isolated . . ." (p. 5). In counterdistinction to such accounts, I would like to foreground all the ways in which these young men themselves defined their lives and their social networks, how their friendship was meaningful to each and both.

LOCATING "HUB CITY"

Rufus and Tony had been childhood friends in Humbrick, having moved to Hub City during the late 1980s. A small Midwestern city, Hub City has a population of over 60,000 and is equally distant from a handful of major cities, including Chicago and Indianapolis, readily accessible via a number of interstate highways from southern states, including Mississippi, Alabama, and Tennessee. African Americans are the largest single minority group here (nearly 20% of the total city population), though whites overwhelmingly dominate (at nearly 80%). The African-American population has traditionally been highly mobile and often transitory, typically coming from and going to this city for a variety of reasons.

As I demonstrated in *Performing Identity/Performing Culture* (2001a), this is a starkly segregated town. The site of a major university, the town is divided, quite literally, by the railroad tracks. When I first met the unit director of the community center, he commented that while black kids will often be rowdy and even destructive in their own neighborhoods, they are scared to "throw a piece of paper on the floor" in white parts of town. These divisions are psychological as well as physical, reinforced by the "common sense" of both blacks and whites, about who lives where, and where such lines begin and where they end.

Economic promise (real or not) attracted many African Americans to the city. Up through the 1970s, this was a manufacturing town, with a number of major factories. These jobs have largely disappeared, the victims of corporate downsizing. Young people still speak of these jobs as lucrative, however, and the individuals lucky enough to have them as all but wealthy.

Work on the railroad was also another traditional economic incentive for people to move here. In fact, Tony's grandfather, whom I will say more about later, came to the city to do this kind of work. He eventually bought a small house which indicated, for many, the relatively rewarding nature of this work. These jobs, of course, have disappeared completely. In fact, many of Phil's grandchildren, unable to secure such work, have lived in this house at various points in time of need. For many, service-sector jobs in fast food (e.g., McDonald's) and megadepartment stores (e.g., K-Mart), as well as manual labor at the university or local hotels, provide the most common other work opportunities. As a result, young people typically work jobs similar to those of their parents. Salaries here are typically minimum wage (or slightly above), $5.15 per hour in July 1997, with little or no security or benefits.

Fear is also another reason that African Americans have migrated to this city. Traditionally, many left the South fearing racism and racial terrorism. This fear is still a living memory for many, including the unit director who often related stories of racism—both explicit and implicit—in the South. These fears of the South recurred at the community center during a recent proposed visit by the KKK to this neighborhood. Many young people commented that the Klan is still active down South and also spoke of relatives who have experienced the Klan's violence. As one young person commented, "They came from Mississippi or Alabama. . . . They be going around burning houses and stuff, putting people, black people, on crosses and burning the crosses."

More recently, many have expressed a general fear of crime, a fear encouraged by popular media forms that often construct cities as irredeemably violent (McCarthy, 1998). Many children from larger cities have been sent here to avoid violence, especially the gang violence that became pronounced beginning in the 1980s. For example, one staff member in his early 30s told me he left Chicago several years earlier, in the mid-80s. When I asked why, he said, "Mom's thought it was about that time!" He was being recruited by a major gang. One young person who left Chicago to come to the town commented that he left because "my mamma thought this was a nice and quiet place." This young person, who briefly flirted with gangs in the city, commented: "At twelve o'clock, mostly every night . . . on the West Side . . . those gangs gonna be shooting . . . just in the air. It woke me up in my sleep." In a similar vein, one young person commented: "In Memphis, if you wear a starter coat, they'll try to take it . . . I been there before and then I saw somebody, they was getting chased and they was like, 'help me, [they] trying to take my coat!' and then they just kept on running and then I had me on one, then I just took off. Zip around the corner." During this discussion, there was a lot of debate concerning which cities were most dangerous. For these youths, this town provided, again, a good and safe alternative.

This city, thus, has an African-American population that migrated here for a variety of reasons, often to leave behind racism, find better jobs, or more recently, to avoid the violence of larger cities. Indeed, young people like Rufus and Tony can often trace their complex family histories across the South and Midwest. Both Rufus and Tony had large families in Humbrick, Mississippi, had grown up there together as small boys. Rufus had three uncles and an aunt still living in this town, all of

Mary's siblings. Tony had a grandmother and several cousins, though all his aunts now lived in "Hub City." Over the few days I visited Humbrick in 1999, I was reunited with several of Tony's cousins, as well as Tony's mother and sister. I also saw several of Rufus's aunts and uncles who I knew from their visits "up North." There was, in fact, a lot of traffic back and forth between these sites. Like many young people today, Rufus and Tony lived their lives in the "in between"—not quite "here," not quite "there." Their notions of the South and the North were continually being revised and revisited—constantly being given new and different meanings dependent upon a whole host of contingencies.

RUFUS

Rufus was born in 1981 and Tony in 1980. Like many young black men, both were closer to their mothers than to their fathers. Indeed, like Tony, Rufus heard several different stories about his father. The one I heard most often was about a man nicknamed "Beretta." Beretta worked in a chemical plant for a while but began dealing drugs and spent some time in prison. His body was ravaged by diabetes and when I finally met him in 1999, he looked much older than his 40 or so years. He was missing nearly all his teeth and—I found out when we shook hands—some fingers. I was surprised when Rufus took me by to meet him. On a trip back South a few years earlier, he had accused Rufus of stealing his hat. Rufus vowed never to speak to him again. However, when Rufus returned for his mom's funeral, which his dad didn't attend, he made a special point of stopping by and seeing if he was hungry, if he wanted some food from the local Burger King.

Rufus spoke with much more clarity about his mother's family. Mary had three brothers and a sister, all of whom still lived in Humbrick. Her dad, Rufus's grandfather, long dead, was a very strict man of apparently mixed parentage. Mary told me she was raised as a "southern lady" which meant deference to her father. She told me one day, after one of Tony's "cousins" had been arrested, that if she ever got in similar trouble, her dad would have come down to the police station with a switch or a belt and have beat her right there. Her dad, very much the patriarch, worked "for the city" as a sanitation man and apparently provided a decent living for his family. However, he always stressed standing on one's own two feet and Mary left Humbrick for "Hub City" at a relatively young age with Rufus to do just that. As Rufus explained it,

> My mom didn't really want me to be around down South. . . . She didn't want me to experience that. She wanted me to see we was equal. . . . We moved up here looking for . . . bigger and better things. . . . Down there, they got a real big problem with poverty. . . . Black people are making a big come up down there but they still living [in] like low, low income homes, stuff like that. And you know, up here, we done came a long way.

He continued,

> We was struggling. So she had signed up for Section 8 . . . [for] something to fall back on. . . . When we first had moved up here we stayed in the projects for a minute but she didn't like that, so she had . . . to work harder. . . . She worked through my godmom [Tony's aunt Shelia]. She had hooked my moms up with a job at the [local hotel] in the laundry room. Since my mom had a real big urge for me not to stay in that environment. . . . So then, after that, through his [Tony's] grandfather, he had gave up his apartment, for my mom to move to their apartment.

While Mary left Humbrick "for bigger and better things," her life was difficult. She worked several jobs, as a cook, in a local hotel, and as a laundress. She soon put her name on a long list for Section 8, public assistance to help subsidize housing, which she eventually got. They lived together, for the remainder of her life, on the bottom floor of a two-family house, on the far reaches of the city, right next to the railroad tracks. The top floor was rented to a rotating series of people, transients who seemed to constantly come and go over the years. At one point, while Mary was quite ill, a very noisy group of older drug addicts and alcoholics lived there. Next door, a family ran a hair salon out of the bottom floor of their home.

Survival was a key theme for Mary and she deployed several such strategies to help make ends meet. She would, for example, let clothes sit in the dryer for several minutes after her time was up, to suck up as much heat as possible. She would, when Rufus was young, strap bag after bag of groceries on his stroller to save on bus and cab fare. Often, she would call on friends and neighbors for rides. She didn't have a car, which became an obsession for Rufus as he became older. Having a car meant freedom from some of life's unpredictable curveballs—whether they came in the form of bad weather or inhospitable relatives. Though often a luxury they could not afford, autonomy was important for both. Indeed, before she died, an insurance man had approached Mary about taking out a policy to help Rufus if she passed away. She sent the man away, telling him, "I taught Rufus how to take care of himself!" Rufus made a special point of telling me how very proud he felt when he heard his mom say this. Self-reliance was an important value for both.

Rufus, by all accounts, was very much a loner from a young age. He spent lots of time at the community center growing up, and grew quite close to all the staff there, including Johnny, the unit director. In fact, some staff members thought that Rufus was abused at home because he never wanted to leave the club when it closed. He would hang out with staff members like Johnny long into the evening, after all the other children had left. Things were often difficult for Rufus as he had no siblings in town, only his mom. He came to look to others for support, just as others looked to him for support. In particular, protection was often difficult to come by and he looked to Tony and his cousins for help. He said,

> Up here, I really don't have no family. I just call Tony and them my cousins 'cause they the closest thing. . . . I'm not safe up here to me, 'cause like when I was coming up, I used to get into fight[s], I was the first one to get jumped, 'cause I ain't have no brothers or no sisters. . . . They always there to back you up. If you had cousins, they was always there to back you up.

Though fragile, this large familial network was very important to Rufus, providing him with a sense of solidarity as well as informal protection in the neighborhood. As I have observed at the club numerous times, young people will almost immediately call on family members to help them deal with interpersonal and potentially violent conflicts. Someone with a large family is privileged in many respects, while someone with a small family is often at a disadvantage. Clearly, Tony and his cousins played an important role in Rufus's life in this regard. They were "the closest thing" he had to extended family in Hub City.

As Rufus grew up, he would maintain all of his allegiances with the "clique" but would also remain a favorite among teachers and staff people alike. While he never did particularly well in school, he participated in many extracurricular activities such as football and did very well in them. Rufus was well-liked by almost everyone with whom he came in contact, especially his teachers, and received a number of awards at the club, including "Youth of the Year." This was a precarious balance. Several of the members of the clique had had trouble with the law, liked to drink, smoke, fight, and "gang bang." Mary often said that she feared Rufus's "cousins" would get him into trouble, which they occasionally, in fact, did.

Rufus thus had to navigate his way between and across several groups—his peers as well as older authority figures. Having made this trip up to Hub City with only his mom, Rufus had to extend his family, which often meant putting his own wants and needs in the background. His personality came to be quite conciliatory, not committing himself wholly to groups of people but always maintaining his distance. This extended to his whole sense of racial and cultural identity: "That's why I try to stay as far away from groups," and, "I try to interact with everybody, 'cause I feel like, I'm not African American, I'm just American." He told me several times that he did not like those boxes that you had to fill in on the SAT which marked you as "black" or "white." He said,

> When I be taking tests, they automatically label you African
> American if you black, if you dark-skinned. Or if you light brown
> skin, they automatically label you Hispanic-American. And I was
> like, "Well how you know I ain't got Greek in my blood, or I
> ain't got Spanish in my blood? French?" You don't ask me that.
> Its just like, I don't see no point for it. Like these SATs and all of
> that. . . . Instead of saying African-American male, why don't you
> just say male such-and-such and have your name. . . . I don't

understand why they gotta have black male and your name and then your age and all of that. I just say American male.

TONY

In many respects, Tony had a very different kind of life than did Rufus. Born around the same time, Tony traveled back and forth for many of his youngest years between Humbrick and Hub City, between the care of his grandmother and his mother. His mom had a rough time early on in Hub City. She had Tony at 16 and another son arrived soon after—then a daughter, then twins, born quite sick. None of the fathers were around for very long and when they were, they didn't provide much support. Tony spent his early years in the projects:

> [The projects] was the worst place I ever lived, man. I ain't have no freedom there. It's like I was a prisoner in my own home. I couldn't go outside 'cause my mom feared I was gonna get shot with a stray bullet. 'Cause it seem like everyday they were shooting out there. They would even go in the buildings and shoot. Only thing I could do was go to the library and straight back home. Library and home. And when I leave the library, I gotta call my mama and tell her I'm on my way home, so she can be watching out for me.

By his own account and the accounts of others, Tony had been something of a nerd growing up. He had big, thick glasses and was exceedingly skinny. When he got older, like many black boys, he felt pressure to conform to more masculinist imperatives and ideals. For Tony, this meant joining a gang.

Gangs in Hub City were offshoots of gangs in nearby Chicago. Throughout the 1960s and 1970s, Chicago was home to gangs such as the Vice Lords, the Blackstone Rangers (soon to be renamed Black P-Stone, then the El Rukens, and then Black P-Stone again), the Latin Kings, the Black Disciples, and the Gangster Disciples (Perkins, 1987). By the 1980s, the top gang leaders (many of whom were then imprisoned) organized all of these factions into two "nations"—the Peoples, or five-point nation; and the Folks, or six-point nation. These two nations served as umbrella organizations for these smaller gangs—the five-point nation included the Vice Lords and Black P-Stone and the six-point nation included the Gangster Disciples (or GDs) and the Black Disciples (or BDs). The former "represents" with the color red, wear their hats cocked to the left, and use a five-point star and crescent as a symbol. The latter represent with blue, wear their hats cocked to the right, and use a six-point Star of David as a symbol. Each had complex institutional histories. Tony spoke about his early decision to join one of the gang "nations" in Hub City:

> When I was younger and I looked at the two gangs and I com-
> pared. I knew eventually when I grew up, I was going to be a part
> of one of them gangs. . . . It's like I figured it out already, 'cause
> of how it was. It was rough. . . . I was about eleven, twelve. I
> look at GDs, and I see like, man, every time you turn around, you
> see a GD fighting a GD, somebody in the six-point fighting each
> other. Now, I said if I do go to the six-point star, I would be a
> BD, because those are the most baddest people that I know under
> the six-point star. They too much don't fight each other. They
> unite more too. And they ain't down with all that gang banging
> stuff. They just on top of their money. That's how it is with Vice
> Lords and Stones to me. They about they money. And when it
> come down to taking care of some business, some dirt, they'll go
> take care of it, get it out of the way, go hide out for a little bit.
> They still stay on top of their paper [money], though. . . . Then
> most of my family was there too. I got family that was Stones,
> Lords, I only have a few, one of my auntie is Queen, Queen GD,
> she Queen Disciple. . . . She got high rank as a female Disciple.
> . . . She here in Hub City, she got out of all that, changed her life
> back around.

Tony's decision to join a gang was multifaceted, informed by his desire for money, for respect, for protection, and even out of family loyalty. Yet, his desire to join a five-point gang was also informed by an impulse—if a misdirected one—for some sort of social or political unity. As Tony noted, the five-point gangs were more likely to "unite" than were other gangs. He said,

Blackstones and Vice Lords, they unite more together than what
GDs and BDs do, you know what I'm saying? I mean, it seems
like all the five-point gangs . . . it seems like they unite better.
And the six-point star gangs . . . GDs, Crips . . . BDs, BGs and all
them, it seem like they don't get along. . . . They fight each other.
Now you go to the city, now, all these five-point gangs don't get
along but when it's time to unite and draw together, go take care
of some business, they'll clique. . . . They believe what Malcolm
say . . . "stop singing and start swinging."

Interestingly, the five-point gangs have a history of organized political activity. In the 1960s and early 1970s, gangs like the Vice Lords
(Dawley, 1973) and the Blackstone Rangers (later Black P-Stone) (Sale,
1971) were involved in many community betterment programs, often
receiving large grants from the government to do so. In fact, the
Blackstone Rangers were, at one point, in discussions to merge with the
Black Panther Party for Self Defense, though discussions eventually
broke down. Still, gangs like Black P-Stone evoked "black power" groups
like the Panthers for many young people, a point driven home in my
weekly discussion groups at the center (Dimitriadis, 2001a). In fact—and
I mentioned this to Tony one day—many young people were drawing
similarities between gangs and the Panthers. He said, "I kinda see where
they [the young people] coming from . . .'cause . . . they see the guns . . .
and they see most gang members with guns, so therefore it put them in
the mind of gangs. And then they got like a little clique and everything
like the gang's got."

Tony had a deep respect for groups like the Black Panthers. In fact,
he obsessively viewed the film *Panther* almost every day for the period
of time we worked together at the community center. He admired the
group's strength, their unity, and their efforts to help others. Tony saw
similar qualities in the Vice Lords. When I gave him a copy of David
Dawley's 1973 book, *Nation of Lords*, which told the story of some of the
Vice Lords's efforts to clean up their community in the 1960s, he read it
voraciously. "Some of these gangs are out there to help," he said. "People
look at gangs nowadays, it's like, 'That's a negative influence, why's you
in a gang?' But some gangs help . . . for instance . . . public service work.
. . . Take the Black Panthers for Self Defense back in the day. . . . They
wasn't about violence. But when it came down to the violence, they take

care of the business." Tony stressed often that he would like to see the gangs in town all come together and do something positive. He said "one day I just want to see all the gangs unite as one powerful and strong thing, like how it was back in the day, with the Black Panthers for Self Defense. That was just one big gang fighting in the streets for equal rights for blacks, along with Martin Luther King and Malcolm." Yet, he realized that this was always difficult, that uniting for some vague notion of "equal rights" usually lost out to more immediate concerns: "Every year something happens, somebody gets shot at, shooting either happens, somebody spraying mace or somebody fighting. Just get to clowning."

Like many young people attracted to gangs, Tony was very self-interested. Tony had a very clear sense of right and wrong—at least on his own logic—and often lost his temper when he felt he had been wronged. This meant, it seemed, an almost never-ending set of confrontations with authority figures in his life—from the police to his teachers to his bosses. Over the years, I heard a seemingly endless series of such stories. The following occurred when Tony called out in the middle of class to correct a teacher. According to Tony, while students always called out in class, the teacher singled him out for misbehavior. He noted:

> We in class and the teacher make a mistake and then I try to correct her . . . and then, you know, she get a little attitude or whatever, you know. I don't appreciate that. I mean, I'm a student, I'm in high school . . . got kicked out of class for correcting a teacher. . . . Basically, the dean gave me an hour detention and I snapped. 'Cause I felt I shouldn't get no detention for trying to correct a teacher. . . . I don't remember what the mistake was, but I just corrected her and out loud. . . . I didn't raise my hand, 'cause most time, we just yell out. So when she kicked me out of class, I went to the dean. I'm pleading my case to him. And pretty much like I told you before—it's like the teacher's always right, the student's wrong. . . . He gave me an hour detention and I felt he was wrong for giving me that, so I snapped on him. . . . I told him, "Man you how you gonna give me an hour detention for something stupid." . . . Basically he suspended me, two weeks.

Tony thus felt that an injustice had been done to him and he "snapped," as he often did. Tony's clear, or perhaps overdetermined, sense of right and wrong marks most of his narratives about such incidents, incidents where he butted heads with authority figures in his life.

Yet gang life had its costs as well. Over the years, Tony spoke often of the risks of gangs—the physical risk, the risk of jail or probation, the constant mind-numbing psychological stresses. Even as they offered key kinds of support and resources, Tony tried again and again to distance himself from their pressures, to remove himself from these networks. The clique, of course, was key in this regard.

THE CLIQUE

Rufus and Tony, again, were close friends, calling each other "cousins." Along with several of Tony's relatives, and (more tangentially) neighborhood friends, this made up what both called "the clique." For these young men, "the clique" was an informal term they used to label this group, to give it some shape and coherence, while also distinguishing it from local gangs. This is critical. Gangs exerted many intense demands, pressures, and risks, and also implied allegiances to individuals one might never have met, to organizations that extended beyond one's local neighborhood. The "nation" imagery used by the five- and six-point gangs (or "organizations") was unambiguous on this point.

The clique, however, was rooted more clearly in the specificities of neighborhood pride, and also, by extension, a sense of southern community. When discussing a favorite hip hop song, "Serious," Rufus noted: "I relate to that one because he's saying how things were in his neighborhood and how he gonna stick with his neighborhood. The neighborhood makes the person, stuff like that. I felt that, 'cause I love my neighborhood. All my friends and stuff." While they both stressed that the clique is not a gang and they do not "claim" territory as does a gang, they explicitly shared fond memories of growing up together here and were very clear about the boundaries and borders of their neighborhood. Part of their investment in their neighborhood was due to safety issues, the fact that their parents wanted them to stay in the neighborhood, where they could be observed. Rufus said, "Remember when we told you how it was a neighborhood thing? Our parents knew we never been no farther than our neighborhood. So it was like, 'Go ahead and let them [play], they ain't going nowhere.' . . . We was always with each other. We never really separate." Rufus said, "Remember when I told you our boundaries was 31st Street . . . to uh, about what 36th or 35th Street all the way to Cobalt and Main Street . . . this whole area provide everything we need." Tony elaborated, "The stores, the money, basically everything, you know what I'm saying? It's the hood," to which Rufus added, "the club."

The clique was key to both Rufus and Tony, an informal social organization that provided an alternative to gang life. While Rufus was never involved in gangs, the clique offered a clearly identifiable family-like support structure in a town where he had only his mom. For Tony, spending more time with the clique allowed him to distance himself from the pressures and demands of the gang life he was enmeshed in. In both cases, the clique was a key source of support marked as different from ever-present gangs, tied to the particularities of their neighborhood and, by extension, the southern town where they had all grown up. Rufus said, "It's just the way it is. [The clique] come before anything else. It's just like when you clique, that's your thing." Tony noted that if "some of my gang members supposedly jumped on Rufus and he was in a different set, I'm gonna go help Rufus, get my gang members up off of him. 'Cause, he's my clique."

Like typical gangs, however, the clique was dominated by young men. While group boundaries were fluid, and both had several female cousins, they didn't seem at all like integral parts of the group. This was clearly a male space, reinforced by constant talk about teen girls and relationships. In particular, "playing" was a notion these young men drew on to talk about romantic relationships, in which manipulation for sex and money and affection was the seeming ultimate ideal and hurt and loss were always at risk. Talk about playing, I found, was a way to mitigate against the very real personal risk that intimate relationships always seemed to imply for these young people—though it is critical to note that playing never implied mental or physical coercion for sex. As much as anything, talk about playing was about marking the borders of this masculinist space. All such relationships were taken very seriously by these youth in the clique.

Tony evokes the fragility of playing, when he notes: "To be a player, you can never like your females . . . well, you can like them but you should never fall for them." The problem, of course, is that the one female you "fall for" might be "playing you." Women, in fact, could be better "players" than men—another constant source of talk. Real commitment, it seems, could only be negotiated over time. Indeed, both Tony and Rufus talked at various points about "giving up playing" when they found a young woman they felt they could trust. "I ain't really tripping off [trying to play] her," Tony said of one young woman, "I respect [her] because of the way she treated my mom." This girl had asked to take Tony's mom out for dinner. Romantic relationships, too, were seen as alternatives to the kinds of illegal and physically dangerous activities associated with gang life and they were a constant subject of discussion within the clique.

FINAL THOUGHTS:
BEYOND "GOOD" VERSUS "BAD" YOUTH

In closing, Rufus and Tony worked to redefine simple notions of good versus bad youth through their friendship. As noted throughout, traditional ideas about success and failure tend to be fairly prescriptive and narrow, laying out seemingly divergent and mutually exclusive pathways for youth. This is particularly true, I think, for young black men, who live with a very debilitating set of social expectations and stereotypes, and in everyday circumstances often fraught with material, physical, and psychological dangers. "Success" often means isolating oneself from others, pulling away from the dangers of unpredictable and often pernicious social networks. We saw this, as noted, in Ron Suskind's *Hope in the Unseen*, which traced Cedric Jennings's social isolation as he moved on to an Ivy League college. "Failure," in turn, often means falling prey to the lure of "peer pressure," the "brotherhood ideology" that marks nearly all accounts of gang life. The clique, as I've shown, was another response, a unique response that looked beyond these often debilitating binary oppositions.

It is difficult, however, to talk about this kind of support and the meanings attached to this friendship in the abstract. The following chapters trace how these modes of affiliation and association unfolded in their lives, across different institutions and sites, in their everyday activities. The following chapters trace "the work" Rufus and Tony did together, surviving and supporting each other as they made the difficult transition to adulthood.

Thinking Beyond
Traditional Schooling:
The Case of Community-Based
Organizations

In the last chapter, I discussed the way Rufus and Tony worked to create and sustain important modes of association and affiliation in their everyday lives. In this chapter, I discuss how their friendship unfolded in the local community center referenced earlier, how this institution enabled their friendship to proliferate in important ways. I begin with a look at several key moments in their lives, at the center.

SCENES FROM A
COMMUNITY CENTER

Just before the summer of 1997, Johnny offered me a staff position at the community center (or "club") where I had been conducting this research. Bill, the education director, suggested it, noting that I had been doing so much volunteer work—answering phones, watching the main game room, and so on—I should be getting paid for it. The offer was—without question—a big honor. Moving from a "researcher" to a "staff" role implied new kinds of responsibilities to the site, its members, and the community (Dimitriadis, 2001b). Indeed, by the time this invitation was made, I had come to see the club as more than simply a place to access young people and conduct focus group sessions. The club and its staff members, I saw, played key roles in the lives of many youth I worked with, including Rufus and Tony.

Youth of the Year

I begin with Rufus's own words, delivered as a speech at the annual Youth of the Year competition held that spring:

> The club means the world to me. First, it is a shield. It blocks negative things from affecting me and other club members. It gives us a safe environment. I get love, enjoyment, and support from the club and staff. It shows me the way to success and how to succeed. Without them, there would be no me.
>
> If it was not for the club, I would probably be a criminal. There are many negative influences around me. But the club has molded me into a strong, powerful, confident, and caring person. Because of them, I have set positive goals. I want to work with kids some day, like my role models at the club. To do this, I must attend college. The club helped me visit Midwest State University [pseudonym] last summer through Partnership for Excellence. The club made me see what I will need to do to get there, like get high grades and do my best in different activities, like the junior varsity football team and my school's "Future Educators" club.
>
> The club and staff are my second family. There are many troubled spots in my first family. I have dealt with poverty, illness, and stress. The club has helped me out through thick and thin. It gives me an environment where I am free to do things like play games, relax, work with computers, and participate in fun and educational programs. For example, I have been in the Eagle Club and also Project Examine. In Project Examine, I developed and played educational games about science and computers.
>
> The club means so much to me. It provides just about everything I could imagine. I love the club and try to give back to it anyway I can.

On this April afternoon, Rufus spoke personally and passionately about the club staff ("without them, there would be no me"), his personal life ("there are many troubled spots in my first family"), his future ("I want to work with kids some day"), and his ethic of community ("I . . . try to give back to it anyway I can"). He even gently played off stereotypes about black males ("If it was not for the club, I would probably be a criminal"). Though there were two other competitors, Rufus won easily. This was not surprising. The club (in general) and Johnny (in particular) recognized Rufus as a kind of quintessential "good kid"—someone who might have taken the wrong road, but was now on the right one, due to the club's influence. He would play this role for the club many times—for visiting reporters, potential donors, and others. Rufus always knew just the right things to say, as demonstrated by his speech that afternoon.

Both Rufus and Tony lived—or "stayed," as they put it—close by this club. Along with his mother and three siblings, Tony lived in a small one-bedroom house right across the street. Just three blocks further, on the first floor of a two-story home, Rufus stayed with his mother. The club—a modern, red brick and glass building—was a centerpiece of this small, lower-income neighborhood. Originally housed in an old school on an adjacent street, the club had moved location about 10 years earlier. Though this newer club had a larger gym, a computer room, and many other more modern features, many claimed to prefer the older building. No one, however, ever questioned that the same powerful ethic—an ethic of community, of responsibility to others—pervaded both spaces.

I had worked with Rufus on his speech earlier in the week. He had even come to visit my basic "public speaking" course on campus to practice in front of an audience. He wanted to do a good job—for Johnny and also for his mother Mary. Mary was quite overweight—a problem compounded by her diabetes—and didn't leave the house very often. She spent most of her days being overwhelmingly exhausted. She would, however, make the trip to the club for the event. She wouldn't, she told me, "miss it for anything in the world." It had been a trip well worth taking. After her son's victory, we all celebrated—Rufus, his competitors and their families, the staff, and others in the audience—with a buffet supplied by Kentucky Fried Chicken. We discussed the upcoming state competition that Rufus would go to the following month, which was the next step before the final, national competition. No one could imagine any other youth winning any of these contests.

Towards the end of the large meal, Mary asked Johnny what the club was going to do with the remaining food. Could she take the leftovers? Johnny said she could take it all, along with some doughnuts we had snacked on earlier. Mary, I would come to see, was always on the lookout for ways to help make ends meet. Rufus immediately suggested, however, we take at least some of it over to Tony's house. Mary didn't object. I followed. I had never been inside Tony's house, though I saw it every day I came to the club. Tony's brother Rick answered the door. He seemed smaller than usual. The hard, rigid countenance he wore at the club was gone. He said very softly, "You can come in." Tony was at work and I was quiet. "This is my family," Rufus said, gesturing towards Tony's mother, brothers, and sister.

We settled down into chairs and began chatting about Rufus's victory and (in particular) his speech, which had been so impressive. At one point, Rufus told Tony's mother Jackie that I wanted to involve Tony in my project on young people and popular culture. I had been having one-on-one interviews with Rufus for a few weeks, when he suggested I also speak with his "cousin," Tony. I agreed, of course. Jackie seemed glad: "Anything to keep him off these streets and out of trouble." Tony had, in fact, shown her the permission form I had given him a few days earlier. Jackie told me that Tony, clearly in a "problem space," had faced a lot of peer pressure early in his life—a familiar theme—and succumbed to it. She offered a seemingly minor but telling example. Tony's eyesight was bad and he had been prescribed a pair of glasses when he was younger. But he had again and again refused to wear them. She said the first pair was "from the government" and looked funny. Refusing to wear them was understandable. But the ones he got later from the Rotary Club, Jackie said, looked very nice. He still, however, feared he might be laughed at, that he might not fit in. So seemingly minor and typical, succumbing to this kind of peer pressure had much wider implications. For Tony, fitting in meant the gang involvement, which overtook his youth and continually threatened his future. Spending time with "an older person—a positive older person"—especially one from the club—could only help.

Rufus was the focus of much "positive" attention that afternoon. Of course this intense focus on him threw into sharp relief those young people who did not manage to resist the "negative" temptations of the street—young people like Tony. Perhaps predictably, this binary logic would always make Rufus very uncomfortable. Indeed, a few weeks later, the local newspaper interviewed Rufus and ran a story about the club and also his victory at the competition. The article was accompanied by a photo of Rufus and also a young girl, Sara, using a computer. During one of our regular interviews, I brought along a copy to perhaps discuss it. To my surprise, Rufus pushed it away. "Get that thing out my face," he said.

Taken aback, I asked him why he didn't like it. How should it have been different? Pointing to the photograph of Sara, he said, "I probably woulda did more on [her]. . . . Just look like some small little portion on her." Noting again how much focus was on him, he said, "Teachers put it in my face, public aide people, people grandmas, and mamas, and aunties, and uncles, cousins, friends. . . . Everybody making a big deal. . . . Everybody's like, 'Have I seen this article?' I'm like 'Everyday.' . . . I ain't never read it. . . . I just glanced at it." He said he would not have done the interview, if Johnny had not asked him. He did not like being singled out as a "good kid" in distinction to other "bad kids." Though he understood that these competitions and stories were necessary to publicize the club, he did not like the attention, did not like being "graded . . . better than the next man." Still, he was willing to do whatever was necessary to help out. Like he said in his speech, he loved the club and tried to give back to it any way he could.

"I'm not the person I want to be"

Like many, Tony admired his best friend Rufus. But it was not the simple admiration of a "feel-good" newspaper article. Fostered through years of friendship, it was an admiration of his continued strength and resilience and it took on new meaning and relevance at this critical juncture in his life. "I got caught up, trying to impress people," he told me, "but Rufus is the one to look up to. Anyone who turns away his friendship is stupid. I'm so glad he won that award." Tony began spending more and more time at the club that spring, as part of his effort, as he put it, to change his "whole environment." "The friends you keep, the people you be around," he said once, "they play an important role. Some of them that I kick it with is negative people and they do a lot of negative things. And so, the way I see it, if I get away from them, get away from the gangs and everything, then I'll be good to go." He recalled moving away from the club a few years earlier, as he got more involved with local gangs. "As I got more into the streets and all that," he told me,

> I started drifting away. [The club] wasn't nothing to me, man. I'm like, "This ain't nothing, man, the streets the bomb." Then I come back, and I look at all these kids, and I tell 'em, I just wanna help

these kids, man. I don't want them to end up out there like me, and a whole bunch of other people out here. All these African-American kids we got in here. I want them to be something positive in this world, not nothing negative.

For Tony, getting away from "the gangs and everything," helping others "to be something positive in this world," meant getting closer to the club and its staff.

But changing one's "whole environment" is easier said than done—a notion starkly reinforced late that April. It was a Tuesday afternoon. Though the club was normally open from 3:00 p.m.–9:00 p.m., we were on a 9:00 a.m.–4:00 p.m. schedule, due to the public school's spring break. I had been at the club since 9:00 a.m. answering phones and organizing some of the memberships for the coming summer rush. I stepped out to run an errand for a staff member around 3:00 p.m. and returned to find Tony badly shaken up, talking intensely and privately with a staff member. Two teens I didn't recognize were in Johnny's office, flanked by Johnny and two other staff members, Bill and Terry. The mood was tense.

I had planned on meeting Tony briefly for an interview before the club closed at 4:00. Although he said he wanted to keep our appointment, I never even got a chance to turn on the recorder. His fear was palpable. Members of a rival gang, Devin and Thomas, had just come to the community center, looking for him. Tony had beaten a friend of theirs a year earlier and they had never forgotten it. The pair had been waiting for a moment of vulnerability and they found it. When they showed up, he had been relaxing, watching television in the "teen center," a small room reserved for teenagers.

The confrontation was over quickly. A relatively new staff member, Claude, spotted the pair and rushed them into Johnny's office. Soon, Bill and Terry were hovering on either side of the teens, while Johnny sat behind his desk admonishing both. They were asked to leave immediately. The incident—the latest in a series—left Tony visibly shaken.

The conflict was complex and dangerous. The two teens had come to Tony's house the day before, armed with pistols, demanding he exit, threatening to enter. Tony's mother had immediately confronted them and told them to leave. They called her a "bitch." Jerry, Tony's cousin, pushed her into the house and stood outside until they left. The encounter had immeasurably aggravated growing tensions between the young men. As Tony made clear, threatening someone's family was "a death warrant." He could never—and he would never—forget it.

Tony, in fact, was far more scared for his family than for himself at this point—scared for his two younger brothers, his sister, and especially for his mother. He feared also for Rufus. Though good in so many ways, Rufus's friendship with Tony and his cousins made him, in the words of Johnny, "guilty by association" for some. Indeed, Rufus had been walking home the previous week, when Devin confronted him. Rufus seemed nonchalant about the encounter, which ended peacefully enough. But it had further enraged and terrified Tony. "I just want it over," he repeated. "I can't take it."

By his own logic, the best possible option for Tony was to fight it out one on one with Devin. And he had driven to their neighborhood earlier to do just that. However, Tony had brought along some of his friends, just in case Devin brought along his, and also brought along a weapon, just in case he did the same. Tony's logic was tightly wound. He came to settle the fight "man to man" and brought his friends and a weapon only in case Devin brought the same. I, of course, had enough perspective on the situation to recognize how flawed this logic was, how showing up in "enemy territory" in a group, armed, would only escalate the situation. Yet, in a situation so volatile, such a change of perspective was simply not possible. When I weakly asked if they could talk it out, he said "ain't no talking to these people."

Such conflicts, I found, were usually elaborate orchestrations of simple fiction, hearsay, rumor, and the like. (This one would be resolved, temporarily, when Tony found out that Devin heard that Tony said he was going to jump him; "he said, she said," Tony said of the tensions that led to the preemptive strike.) However, at moments like this, their consequences could not be any more real, both physically and psychologically. I had seen firsthand how paranoia could ravage Tony, how living in constant fear for his well-being and the well-being of those around him could dissemble his mental landscape. I noticed, when we first began spending time together, how he never focused for too long on any one thing. Any passing car, any passing person, became the focus of rapt suspicion for several intense seconds. Anyone and anything was quite simply a threat until proven otherwise.

Tony told me he was strongly into street life "for three years" as we sat in the back of the community center late that afternoon. "I woke up every morning scared, thinking about who's out to get me, whose going to jump me, whose corner I'm on." All this, of course, was a part of living gang life—the other side to the image of invulnerability these young men often portrayed to those around them. Though in many ways still trapped in this life and its logics, it was a life that Tony—at 17—was growing tired of. Turning his life around meant turning to the club—for safety, for peace, for a sense of performing well in an important, local institution. "I ain't ashamed to say it," he told me, "but sometimes when I think about how bad I messed my life up, I just cry. I ain't ashamed to say it, but sometimes I just lay in bed crying." His fear, it seemed, had clarified something about his life so far: "I'm not the person I want to be."

THE CLUB: POTENTIAL AND POSSIBILITY

I begin here with a basic proposition. Community-based organizations such as the club are key, alternative educational sites that are serving important roles and functions for a broad spectrum of disenfranchised youth in ways we are only beginning to understand. As evidenced by the "scenes" from the community center explored above, the community center played very different though often complementary roles for Rufus and Tony. For Rufus, the club and the staff were (among other things) his "second family," one that helped him deal with the "troubled spots [in his] first family." For Tony, the club provided him with a protected space to reimagine himself at a critical and dangerous juncture in his life. For each, the club offered a complex and contradictory terrain, one that challenged and exceeded the narrow confines into which they were so readily cast. Each had a kind of "success" at this club that they did not have at school—a success realized (as I will show) when they eventually took coveted staff positions.

Life in School and at the Club

Scholars such as Shirley Brice Heath, Milbrey McLaughlin, Lois Weis, Michelle Fine, and their colleagues have begun recently to explore the importance of out-of-school learning sites (Dimitriadis & Weis, 2001; Fine & Weis, 1998; Heath, 1996; Heath & McLaughlin, 1993, 1994; McLaughlin, Irby, & Langman, 1994; Weis & Fine, 2000). As a result of "alternative" life courses, these writers show that marginalized young people like Tony and Rufus often develop sets of skills valued in their local community and at community-based organizations, but not always in school. These organizations give voice to the complexity of their lives and struggles in a way that school does not.

In particular, both Rufus and Tony saw schools as places where they were continually divided and sorted out into meaningless categories. Tony, for example, was labeled as a "special education" student from a young age. "I used to play along with them," he told me. "'Cause that's how you get through the school easier. The work is much easier. You know, it's like going to easier classes." But, he also told me, "I'm a smart kid. I know I'm smart." It was only when he was sent to a local alternative school and was allowed the freedom to work at his own pace on projects, that he realized he liked to learn. "But right now at [this school] I see how much more I excel and how much fun I had with it, like Pre-Trig . . . that stuff was crucial. I liked doing that stuff, 'cause it worked my brain. It was a challenge." Traditional school, unfortunately, rarely provided such challenges. Most often, school meant having only to defer uncritically to teachers who treated him like a child and perform rote and meaningless tasks.

Rufus expressed similar frustration with school and its hierarchies. In particular, Rufus was frustrated with the constant impulse (as noted) toward the kind of multifaceted "grading" which was so especially apparent in school. He told me, "I'm getting tired of being graded lesser or better than the next man." He continued, talking about the traditionally defined aspects of grading, "When we go to school, they always talking about, 'Why you doing so bad?' It's like, 'I'm learning something, [so what's the difference?].' But then, everybody always look at your grade. Give you a piece of paper. They go by what's on the piece of paper." He went on to talk about how meaningless these distinctions can be in other areas as well. "I don't care if it was [grade] one through five, one through three . . . If you ate your cookies in preschool sloppy . . . they say you was a sloppy little kid, which is grading you better or worser."

Community centers such as this one, however, tend to operate on a different, less strictly hierarchical model. For example, the ability to manage multiple, authentic tasks, to learn new tasks quickly, to work in het-erogeneously aged groups, and to work under pressure are skills critical to the functioning of these sites. These are skills, it is important to note, many young men like Rufus and Tony must hone out of material necessi-ty, often as a result of their urgent contributions to maintaining function-ing households—something Tony and Rufus understood quite well. These organizations are places where many such teens can shine, in ways they cannot in school, allowing them to translate a different kind of cul-tural capital into an alternative kind of success.

Working at the Club

Though I came to this center in 1995 to study young people and their relationship to and with popular culture, I began performing volun-teer work there during the spring of 1997 and was (as noted) offered a staff position for the summer of 1997 (see the appendix as well as Dimitriadis, 2001b). In addition to the fact that I was putting in so much volunteer time, Bill, the education director, also thought that I would be a logical choice to help organize educational activities for club members. Since I was pursuing a doctorate in speech communication, he suggested I might be able to organize a debate team. He stressed that some of the worst-behaved kids were leaders and just needed some guidance. This clearly was the case for Tony, whom Bill wanted to move, along with Rufus, into a junior staff position for the coming summer. Like many staff members at these organizations, Bill often gave trouble-prone youth more responsibility instead of less responsibility as a pedagogical tactic or strategy.

Both Rufus and Tony worked at the club that summer through a pro-gram called TAWC (Teens at Work in the Community). Johnny was gear-ing Rufus for a position at the club and had contacted those involved with the program about his coming to work there. Johnny saw him as a "natu-ral" for the position. He was, however, less enthusiastic about Tony. Though Johnny had known Tony nearly all his life and genuinely liked him, he knew of his history of gang involvement and feared he would bring problems to the club. Indeed, early in June, Tony's cousin had a very violent conflict with another young man, Terry, near the club—just the latest in a seeming endless series of events. When Johnny heard that Tony was trying to get a job at the club through TAWC, he was wary: "I like Tony, but there is a reality to the situation." At Bill's continued prompting, however, Tony did get the position. However, Johnny told him in no uncertain terms at the beginning of the summer, "Keep your friends away from the club." Knowing Rufus's home life was filled with potential demands and pressures, he told him, "Keep your home life away from the club."

I was asked to organize activities in the multipurpose room that summer. Tony was assigned there along with me. (I have, as such, more firsthand knowledge of his experiences over this 3-month period.) The multipurpose room was a large open room with collapsible tables and chairs. We served hot lunch in this room. Coordinating meals and cleaning up afterwards was part of my job as well. The multipurpose room was one of five areas at the club. The other four areas were designed for more specific activities. The games room (in many respects the club's "main area") had a Ping-Pong table, three pool tables, a hockey table, and a Nintendo game set. The gym, in turn, had all kinds of sports equipment that young people could use. Finally, the arts and crafts room and the library were stocked with art equipment, books, and computers, all of which could be used creatively by young people and staff members. Rufus was assigned to watch the games room on a daily basis, along with another staff member.

I tried, at least initially, to hold onto my research design on the topic of young people and popular culture. While I could not conduct focus groups over the summer, I thought it would be a good time to do more personal one-on-one interviews. I agreed to put in an extra 2 hours a day of unpaid work to justify the time I would take to conduct these sessions. The plan was, at relatively calm moments, to take a free room and talk with a few different young people for a half-hour or so. In particular, I had planned to conduct a series of one-on-one interviews with a teen girl, Cheryl, that summer. I had already conducted a few such exploratory sessions with Cheryl, and planned to use that summer to collect more specific biographical material. Perhaps erroneously, perhaps not, I felt that these interviews would need to be done at the club. While I could spend time with young men like Tony and Rufus outside the club, I felt uncomfortable spending such private time with teen girls. My role in the community was ever-scrutinized—I had to make decisions about what was and what was not appropriate. Again, if I was to interview Cheryl, I thought, it would have to be at the club.

Yet, as one might expect, we were understaffed and always in the middle of a crisis and I was always needed for some very immediate purpose. These interviews quickly became untenable. This was quite unfortunate, as I was never privileged to the same kind of rich, long-term personal material on teen girls that I was on teen boys like Rufus and Tony. More specific biographical material on young woman—or even a single young woman—would have highlighted, I am sure, a distinct and perhaps overlapping set of gender dynamics that would have proven quite illuminating.

My relationship with Tony and Rufus, however, deepened immeasurably over this summer. We now, as I will note, were working together side by side in a difficult, though very rewarding, job. We often went for food after work or we often hung out—time permitting—during lunch. We often went shopping together, did errands around town, and so forth. We were in frequent and familiar contact.

The Games Room

I am not sure exactly why the decision was made to have Rufus watch the main floor—but I suspect it was because the role was appropriate for someone with his disposition. Watching the games room demanded staying in the background, remaining low-key, and mediating the disputes of young people on a case-by-case basis as they played various games like Ping-Pong and pool. Importantly, it was almost impossible to micro-manage young people here, as rules to these games were cocreated in moment-to-moment and often unpredictable fashion. I learned this with time. From the very first night that I had volunteered to work the games room floor 4 months earlier, I was struck by the number of small conflicts—from shouting to slight pushing—that would erupt around these games. My initial response was largely reactive. I would immediately ask what was wrong. I could almost never figure out exactly what the issues in dispute were—someone would complain that someone else was "practicing too long" or "volleying on five instead of two." I usually just said that everyone should simply stop arguing—a poor response, which left the question of who was wrong and who was right unanswered. With time, and as I learned the subtleties of these games, I began giving club members more space to work these kinds of disputes for themselves, only interfering when a rule was clearly being broken or a physical fight seemed immanent.

One had to be very sensitive in this regard, I learned, to know where and when to assert oneself and when and where to let young people work it out for themselves. One had, as well, to learn the difference between club rules and young people's self-generated rules "in play." For example, when playing Ping-Pong, young people balanced the twin goals of winning the game fairly and extending time at the table. Since the club was usually crowded, with more youth than tables, the staff designed a method to keep time allotted fairly. The winner of any particular game would play the next person in line at that table, who called "downs," which means "I play next." If you left the table (even to go to the bathroom) you lost your "downs." This rule was meant to prevent young people from going from table to table and calling "downs" indiscriminately.

Young people also generated their own rules to serve their needs and interests. For example, young people would first practice for a while, perhaps a minute or two. Practicing could be extended, if participants agreed, to further time spent at the table, especially if lots of people were waiting. Players could say they needed more time to work on their game, though sometimes other people complained about this. Players would then "volley," which means playing to see who gets to serve first. Volleying can be based on scoring two points or five points. It is, in large measure, up to the participants. Practicing and volleying were two strategies young people used to extend their time at tables. However, you can't win a game by simply extending time noncompetitively. So, there was a constant tension between winning and extending the game as long as possible. Similar dynamics work across a number of games, including pool and table hockey—all of which were enmeshed in young people's own, self-generated rules that all needed to be monitored by a staff member.

Rufus was able to occupy this role quite well. He was aloof enough to allow young people to manage their own games, though was able to step in when necessary to enforce the spirit of the rules if not the letter. This was often difficult. For example, there was a rule that you "lost your downs" if you touched the table while others were playing. This was to prevent purposeful distractions. However, at several points, young people would (in fact) accidentally touch the table and others, perhaps wanting to move up in line, would demand they lose their turn. Such decisions were difficult and Rufus stressed to me how he learned how to discipline fairly over time, to judge the spirit over the letter of the rules. He agreed that these rules often took on a rigidity and life of their own: "I think I discipline some of them for petty reasons . . . like touching the table deal. That became a big problem." Rufus, like a good educator, worked on this problem and was considered quite successful in this role, able to enforce rules with a degree of fluidity and sensitivity.

The Multipurpose Room

The room that Tony and I worked in, the multipurpose room, was much less structured and demanded that we design and implement more specific kinds of activities. The room was appropriate for Tony, as his was a much more forceful personality—someone willing to put forth his opinions and ideas—someone who clearly saw himself and was seen by others as something of a leader. Much of the expectation early on was that we would conduct more formal kinds of whole-group educational activities. These included Good Moves and Talking with CJ, activities that tried to teach young people certain kinds of life skills. For example, Good Moves was a program designed to give youth scenarios and then ask them if particular choices were "good moves" or not. These programs tend to be very popular with upper administration—they were offered in different community centers and were modeled on principles deemed effective across different sites. As noted, I was hired (in part) on the assumption that I would be able to organize such activities.

While these kinds of programs were valued by the administration, they were very difficult to orchestrate in practice, and tended not to resonate with group members. I found it extremely difficult to do whole group activities of any kind and I wound up in more of a disciplinary role than was appropriate. The first few sessions—especially with the early adolescents—descended quickly into chaos and I was reprimanded several times for my lack of control. In fact, I turned to Tony for help early on and suggested—both to give him a model and because I thought it would be interesting—that he try to run the group the way I ran my discussion groups on popular culture. He agreed and opened the first such session by announcing that we were going to "do some black history." He then corrected himself and said "some *good* black history." He was armed with two videos—a documentary about Malcolm X and the film *Panther*, both of which I had given him while he was participating in the focus groups mentioned. He showed the Malcolm X video this first session, asking questions like, "Who was Malcolm X?" and "What's a Muslim?" He then talked a little about how the black Muslims believed in "swinging, not singing," and also talked about how the Panthers believed the same thing. Interestingly, these facts were all gleaned from the popular films with which he was so familiar.

It is crucial to note here how easily Tony was able to enact a "teacherly" persona. As noted, Tony had nothing but trouble with teachers in school, was suspended several times, and eventually had to leave for an alternative, local school. Yet here he was able to embody this role quite effectively—asking questions of the "class," separating young people who were misbehaving, saying things like, "Do you want to share what you're saying with the class?" Of course, Tony was parroting here, at least in part, some of the ways that his teachers talked in school. Yet at the same time, Tony was also very self-conscious about resisting the kinds of interactions and power dynamics modeled for him at school.

Much of his willingness to work to embody a pedagogical role had to do with how authority was perceived to operate at the club. Specifically, the negotiated kind of authority at work at the center was more appealing to Tony than the kind effected at school. In fact, he repeated, as did many young people, that in school, the teacher alone decides who was right and who was wrong. At the club, however, "You always have a chance to tell your side of the story." In fact, at the end of the summer, when I asked Tony if working with young people made him sympathetic to his teachers, he said "No!" quite vehemently—that if nothing else, it told him just how unfair his teachers and his school really were.

This more flexible ethos allowed many different kinds of creative activities to take place at this site. For example, a few days following the discussion of Malcolm X, Tony suggested we discuss whether the evidently murdered rap star Tupac Shakur was really dead or whether he had faked it—a very heated topic at this time (Dimitriadis, 2001a). Tony, at this point, believed that Tupac was alive and asked these young people to support or defend their different positions on the subject. As the conversation progressed, the group got a little wild and he immediately asked, "Do y'all want to watch the Malcolm X video?" He sensed—before I did—that there was little interest in this documentary and used it as leverage against the group. When interest seemed to wane further, he suggested another activity. Tony, interestingly, used the space we had to organize a dance contest and helped different young people find different ways to participate in it. He had some young people (particularly girls) self-generate into dance groups and come up both with choreographed routines and colorful names like Ms. Thang, All That, and Tha Starz. He had others serve as judges, others work the radio, and still others (particularly boys) act as "security." The idea was brilliant (I never would have thought of it) and we used it several times over the course of the summer.

For the next several weeks, we worked together with intensely energetic young people to find sets of activities that they would find most appealing. The whole-group activities by and large failed, but we did find ways to give young people sets of options and create the contexts where they could engage with them. We provided decks of cards, box radios, jump ropes, videos, and even (yes) pen and paper to write stories. Even here, Tony felt his way into a pedagogical role, in very interesting ways. I recall an afternoon session in July, working with 11- and 12-year-olds—a particularly difficult group.

We began by giving the group choices about what they could do—play cards, jump rope, and so on. I also mentioned that we were starting a "wall of writing" in the games room and said that if anyone would like to write something, we would display it. Most of the youth chose to play games like jumping rope or playing cards, while six wrote essays. We took this group to a more private table, and handed out pens and pencils. I asked what everyone would like to write about. There was little response. Responding to the pause, Tony quickly keyed the discussion in a more specific way, asking, "What's wrong with your neighborhood?" The group perked up. One girl said that the parks around were in bad shape and when they were "repaired" they were only painted over. None of the broken-down benches or swings were ever replaced. Another girl said that there needs to be more "protection" for houses and businesses. I asked if the police were the answer and they all said unequivocally, "No."

Tony asked, "Who heard about the shooting in the papers?" All said they had. "The neighborhood was calm," he said, "but now the police are all over the place." Recalling the story mentioned at the outset of this chapter, he said, "Someone came to my house looking for me and the police never came when my mom called." "Where were they then?" he asked. One of the girls mentioned "neighborhood watches" and asked if they were still around. Everyone said no. Some of the girls then mentioned gangs and drugs. Tony quickly turned the conversation to some of the personal problems he had had. He said that he used to "do dirt" and talked about how hard that life was. Again, recalling our earlier discussion, he said, "You don't know who you're dealing with or whose corner you're working on." He said that he had been on probation since 1993 and "it was hell."

Tony continued, noting that he had "enemies all over the city looking for him"—the paranoia evidenced in April, turned into a pedagogical resource. One of the girls mentioned Terry, the young man with whom Tony's cousin had had the conflict. Tony said that Terry was "one of [his] enemies" and the person who injured him was his cousin. This discussion ended fairly quickly—and I was glad. One of the boys then said that he had been jumped and stabbed and showed a long scar along his forearm. Tony then showed off some of his knife scars.

Talk turned to shared fears. One of the girls said that in the projects, some people "sleep in their bathtubs" because they are afraid to be near vulnerable windows. Tony said that when he lived in the projects, he spent many nights "hiding in the closet." He recalled someone shooting off a Tech-9 in his hallway. "All I could hear that night," he said, "were the gunshots." He said he stayed up all night, thinking they were coming for him. One of the boys, in a seeming nonsequitur, said that there are more blacks in prisons than whites. Tony responded by saying that he was thankful his mom "beat on him" to help keep him in line. If not, he said, he would be in prison right now instead of on probation. Another girl said that the state will come and take you away from your parents if they hit you, "but parents do that," she said, "to help keep their kids out of trouble." The group, for the most part, agreed with this.

Tony understood that this conversation, in all its complexity, was grist for their essays. He did not shy away from the kinds of issues that teachers often shy away from either by choice or decree—the capriciousness of the police, the occasional necessity of fighting, the perceived "need" for corporal punishment in a racist culture, the paralyzing fear of violence. He drew on his own life, as well—his mistakes, his concerns, his fears. He was even able to tread lightly around a set of gang-related tensions he was still (partially) enmeshed in. Towards the end, he said that their writing might even help change how people think and bring about some needed change. The group broke part and everyone worked on their essays.

Tony, thus, was able to draw on young people's interests and work with them in creative ways. This was quite an accomplishment for a 17-year-old who had lain in bed 4 months earlier, crying that he was "not the person that he wanted to be." The club provided Tony with another model for who he might be—a model validated locally by his family and peers. By the end of the summer, he expressed interest in being a teacher, as part of his broader effort to "turn his life around." The club provided him with the opportunity to be creative in drawing on his own skills and interests— skills and interests often elided in traditional schools. The club provided many such possibilities for these young people to perform well and both learned a lot from the experience. As Tony said, "I learned you can't treat kids all the same way. You gotta learn how to work with them. You know what I'm saying, like, remember how we used to make all the kids do everything together? [i.e., play whole-group games and engage in whole-group activities] I learned you gotta divide them up, do different things with different kids." Tony thus learned how to work with youth's interests, treating them as individuals while trying to maintain some kind of order—a remarkable achievement by any standard. Both Rufus and Tony agreed that young people were difficult, but decided over the summer that all were basically good. As Tony summed up, "Nan [not] one of them is bad."

These jobs at the club helped Rufus and Tony to focus their lives in ways school never did—to teach, and to learn how to teach well. These decisions came by way of practical experience. Tony said, "I figured out this summer that a lawyer probably wouldn't be the best job for me. . . . I think teaching probably would be good. I might go to school to become a teacher. . . . A whole bunch of people said I would make a better teacher."

BUMPS IN THE ROAD

As I have shown throughout, the club offered both teens a space to imagine different kinds of lives for themselves in a way school did not, in a way that drew on and validated their complex everyday realities. These kinds of community-based organizations, I argue, have enormous potential for addressing the needs and concerns of disenfranchised youth—a critical and underexplored issue. Yet, at the same time, I do not want to tell a simple, uncritical story about the club "saving" youth. Though this is a compelling narrative (one Rufus drew on at the Youth of the Year competition) it does not speak fully to the complexities of these organizations in relation to young people's everyday lives—a notion also evoked, I hope, in the opening narratives. After the summer of 1997, both were offered more stable staff positions—Rufus, during the fall of 1997 and Tony, during the fall of 1998. But neither held them for very long for specific (if predictable) reasons.

Rufus has always prided himself on being able to get along with anybody. However, the club, during the fall, attracted older members who often came to stay warm. The job came to demand that he discipline his peers who sometimes (for example) came into the club with gang paraphernalia. It was very difficult for him to inhabit this role, and he wound up quitting. Rufus's day-to-day life demanded "being cool" with everyone, at all times, which was simply not possible here. This was an issue, as well, in the national Youth of the Year competition. While Rufus won the local competition (as noted), he was defeated in the state-wide event the following month. Johnny heard later that the interview did not go particularly well. The interviewer, who was white, asked Rufus what he thought of Louis Farrakhan. He faltered, saying only that he was a good speaker. Rufus was always attentive to walking fine social and cultural lines—he simply did not know what to say, could not get a sense of the interviewer's agenda. There didn't seem to be a "right answer" to the question, the way there were "right answers" to other questions.

This was not a problem for Tony who, as mentioned previously, was more used to putting his own sense of self, his opinions, on the line. But Tony had different problems—ones rooted in his absolute sense of right and wrong and his confrontational personality. For example, he came close to having a fist fight with a person doing public service at the club, as this person had used profanity around younger club members. For Tony, it was a question of right and wrong and he invited the transgressor outside to settle it once and for all, with all the children watching. He said, quite clearly, "I don't care if I get fired." Tony's sense of self was at stake here and, again, worked at cross purposes with the institution's imperatives. He left voluntarily but came close to being fired several times. In addition, his personal life—"his friends," as Johnny put it—continued to exert pressure on him. He was never quite able to extricate himself from his social networks, which were enmeshed in local gang culture. Indeed, his conflict with Devin would subside and flare up several times over the years, as it would with other young people—"boys," as he put it, "I'm into it with."

Thus, we see the complex role and importance of this community-based organization in the lives of Rufus and Tony. This organization both validated their experiences, while it was subject to all the real-world issues they invited. I offer this paradox in an attempt to begin a more complex dialogue about these sites and their educative power. Indeed, these sites are not easily assessed with the kinds of tools and measures that would deem them wholly "successful" or not. Rather, they are emergent and unpredictable in all manner and form—reliant on a particular nexus of forces difficult to predict beforehand.

In particular, while neither Tony nor Rufus stayed long at the job, it allowed both to accrue different kinds of rewards, both tangible and intangible. On the one hand, it offered them both experience that translated into resume-building capital, capital that helped Rufus focus his postcollege endeavors (including getting into a competitive college preparatory program) and helped Tony to get off of probation. On the other hand, it gave them both the more intangible experience of succeeding, for at least a time, in coveted authority roles. In particular, being a teacher is now and forever a key part of their imaginative landscape, linked to the senses of self they are capable of conjuring up in the face of adversary or challenge. This will be made exceeding clear in the final chapter, I hope, which discusses how both dealt—individually and together—with the vicissitudes of their postteen years. These were (and are) years of struggle—struggle with employment, with the idea of future fatherhood, with alcohol, with violence, with friendship. This "imagined self" of "teacher" served as a key mooring in a world that seemed at points at best indifferent to their lives and their well-being.

FINAL THOUGHTS

As Penelope Eckert (1989) argues, schools typically operate on "corporate models" that divide young people, atomize their roles, and encourage them to move ahead in a lateral, hierarchical fashion. A strict split between in-school and out-of-school relationships is fostered. Less privileged youth, however, operate on a very different model. This is a more collaborative and supportive model, one that encourages heterogeneous relationships that coexist between and across institutions. Eckert calls, as such, for an education that is based on real-world activities that can draw on all the resources such young people bring to the table—resources often ignored in school life. In many respects, current work on community-based organizations stresses similar concerns and develops a similar model, highlighting the resources and collaborative networks young people bring to these organizations as they engage in real-world activities (Heath, 1996; Heath & McLaughlin, 1993, 1994; McLaughlin, Irby, & Langman, 1994).

Recent work by Weis and Fine (2000) has also extended this discussion to include the "free spaces" young people carve out for themselves inside of traditional educative sites. In particular, Weis and Fine's notion of "free spaces" highlights much of the imaginative work young people invest in, creating "spaces" out of the "places" made available to them in the quotidian. "Young men and women," they write, "are 'homesteading'—finding unsuspecting places within their geographic locations, their public institutions, and their spiritual lives to sculpt real and imaginary corners for peace, solace, communion, personal and collective identity work. These are spaces of deep, sustained community-based educative work, outside the borders of formal schooling" (Fine, Weis, Centrie, & Roberts, 2000, p. 132). Such sites provide ways for young people like Rufus and Tony to "reimagine" what education might mean—where it takes place and what their role in it might be.

I have elaborated on these ideas throughout this chapter, stressing the productive nature of these sites, how they allow young people to succeed in ways typically not encouraged in school. I have also showed how "success" is uneven, difficult to reproduce, and often fleeting. This kind of "success" is often very difficult to assess. I will pick this theme up in the next chapter, as much of this had to do with key staff members, including Johnny, an important older figure in both their lives. These sites require the consistent presence of skilled older people or "wizards" who serve multiple and various roles (Heath & McLaughlin, 1993). These "wizards," McLaughlin and colleagues write, "have created environments in which youth from the tough streets of inner-city neighborhoods can imagine a possible future." The success of these wizards is extremely "difficult to emulate because it is highly personal" (McLaughlin, Irby, & Langman, 1994, p. 37). As they make clear, it is simply not possible to reproduce successful programs in cookie-cutter fashion, as such programs often rely on the highly particular and context-specific work of individuals who have often spent close to their whole lives in these communities and understand their often complex problems, concerns, and values. In many respects, it is difficult to wholly disentangle such organizations from the wizards who conjure them up and make them real in the every day.

CHAPTER FOUR

In the "In-Between": Role Modeling in Urban America Today

Rufus, Tony, and I had spent the summer of 1997 working at the community center. Side by side, we organized and oversaw the activities of a range of young people for three long, grueling months, as detailed in Chapter 3. Now, beginning the fall of 1997, we were all settling down into our different roles. Rufus was attending high school and working at the club; Tony was working at McDonald's and also going to a local alternative high school; and I was back in graduate school, teaching, writing up my doctoral qualifying exams, as well as doing focus groups and also volunteering at the club. I recall a conversation I had with Johnny early that school year. He had some good news. Rufus had started working as a regular staff member that fall and had also joined his high school's Junior Varsity football team. He was excited about both prospects. Johnny saw Rufus as "following in his footsteps," perhaps one day taking over his own job. "Nothing would make me happier," he said. Rufus would continue to look after the games room floor that fall, every day after school.

Johnny was also excited that Rufus would be joining his high school football team. Though Rufus was over 300 pounds and very strong, he was afraid of playing sports, because he was afraid that he would "get hurt." Johnny had encouraged him to go out for football, to help build up his confidence and also his aggressiveness. Rufus had a hard time asserting himself and often tried simply to blend into the background wherever he was. This had all kinds of implications. Johnny, for example, seemed to fear that Rufus would "settle for a general laborer job" when he graduated, that he would not push himself as forcefully as he should.

Football would also help keep Rufus out of trouble. While we were talking, a teenager named Billy walked by. Billy was in a gang. As he passed, Johnny said, only half-jokingly, "Football will keep Rufus away from Billy and his friends, too!" In encouraging him to play football while avoiding gang life, Johnny evoked a tension felt by many black young men—how to assert oneself, to be aggressive, to be "a man," without getting into the kind of trouble that he could not walk away from—the trouble of gang life, of the streets. It was a precarious balance gird by compulsory masculinity, one that black teenagers like Rufus had to walk daily. This was a balance hard to strike in the abstract. It was a balance best embodied in the everyday practices of older men like Johnny, men who maintained respect on the "streets" while connecting to broader kinds of communities as well. Johnny was, in every respect, a role model or mentor for these young men.

This discourse about "mentorship" and "role models" has become increasingly prominent over the past decade—as something of a magic bullet in policy discussions about urban youth. As Joy Dryfoos (1998) writes in *Safe Passage: Making it through Adolescence in a Risky Society*, "We have strong evidence to support that when children are attached to well-trained and supervised mentors, case managers, or older peer tutors, their achievement and academic levels improve" (p. 201). She goes on to note that such individuals can often be found in institutions, including: "Cities-in-Schools, Big Brothers/Big Sisters, Boys and Girls Clubs, Girls Inc., 4H, religious organizations, senior citizen groups, and universities" (p. 201). Providing "role models" to young people is central to the missions of these organizations.

The importance of "role models" is reinforced in popular culture and discourse as well, where it is often explicitly gendered. For example, the well-known film *Boyz 'n the Hood* positions its main character, Furious Styles, as the answer to many of the youths' problems, including those of his teenaged son Tre. It is Furious who teaches Tre "how to be a man," Furious who teaches him about Afrocentrism, Furious who chases a burglar out of their home, gun drawn, Furious who tells Tre to be careful of Dough Boy, the young gang member who lives next door. The importance of positive black male role models is a theme that resonates broadly throughout black popular culture, including in films like *South Central* and *Menace II Society*.

While my own project quite clearly underscores the importance of such relationships, I will try to reposition this discussion in some key ways. In particular, while much of the work on "role models" tends to focus on their "ideal" characteristics, I will focus instead on the work young people themselves do understanding these figures, how they acknowledge and validate this kind of authority and why. As argued earlier, young people like Rufus and Tony have to "grow up fast," often taking on tremendous responsibility from a very young age. Authority for these young men always has to be earned; it is never simply given. Indeed, while Rufus and Tony said they wanted and needed the guidance of those older, they also each said quite clearly and explicitly, "I ain't no shortie [child]." In this chapter, I will tease out some of the implications and contours of this complex and seemingly paradoxical nexus.

I would like to begin by looking at the role and importance of so-called old heads in extant sociological literature.

OLD HEADS

For some time now, sociologists have been concerned with how values are transmitted across generations. Indeed, there is a long and influential body of work by scholars such as William Julius Wilson and Elijah Anderson, which has discussed the ways changing economic conditions have fostered "ghetto-related behavior"—behavior reproduced across generations in marginalized areas. More and more, young people in these neighborhoods are not socialized to operate outside of the "ghetto" but only within it and its own peculiar assumptions and logics. More and more, these neighborhoods are losing the kinds of role models who can help broker more complex and nonlocal cultural transactions.

According to William Julius Wilson (1996), these cultural shifts are rooted in economic devastation. Indeed, Wilson has documented in compelling recent work the economic dislocations that have so clearly enabled new concentrations of urban poor in the United States. As Wilson notes, "The 1970s and 1980s witnessed a sharp growth in the number of census tracts classified as ghetto poverty areas, an increased concentration of poor in these areas, and sharply divergent patterns of poverty concentration between racial minorities and whites"—a trend that has gone unabated (p. 15). This has critical implications for the cultural life of such areas. "Neighborhoods plagued by high levels of unemployment," Wilson writes, "are more likely to experience low levels of social organization" (p. 21).

Neighborhood organization depends upon "the extent of local friendship ties, the degree of social cohesion, the level of resident participation in formal and informal voluntary associations, the density and stability of formal organizations, and the nature of informal social controls" (p. 20). A low level of organization, according to Wilson, has direct implications for the ways children are socialized—if they are socialized to become active parts of a wider, dominant social and cultural milieu or if they are to operate mostly within ghetto-specific parameters. Neighborhoods with strong kinds of organization are able to "supervise and control the activities and behaviors of young people" (p. 20). Old heads are around and have the authority to guide and discipline young people in appropriate ways.

Yet such socialization mechanisms are becoming increasingly scarce. According to Elijah Anderson, once neighborhood cohesion crumbles, "old heads" lose their power and authority with young people. An "old head," according to Anderson (1990), "was a man of stable means who believed in hard work, family life, and the church. He was an aggressive agent of the wider society whose acknowledged role was to teach, support, encourage, and in effect socialize young men to meet their responsibilities regarding work, family, the law, and common decency." However, such models have become increasingly rare, and a new kind of role model has emerged: "young, often a product of the street gang, and at best indifferent to the law and traditional values" (p. 3).

These new role models often socialize young people into what Anderson calls "the code of the street" (1999). This code is one of personal respect, "loosely defined as being treated 'right' or being granted one's 'props' (or proper due) or the deference that one deserves" (p. 33). Yet, in the ever-uncertain contexts in which people find themselves, this notion of personal respect, personal space, becomes uncertain. "Consequently," according to Anderson, "people become very sensitive to advances and slights, which could well serve as a warning of imminent physical attack or confrontation" (p. 34). Here, the streets become a theater where respect is negotiated and brokered on myriad levels—for example, overextended eye contact or control of physical space. All challenges major and minor take on intense significance.

According to Anderson, "ghetto families" socialize their young either to embrace wholly "the code of the streets" or to merely be aware of it and navigate their way around it. The former are what Anderson calls "street" while the latter are "decent." Importantly, survival itself often demands that "decent" folks have to act "street." The webs are as complex, intricate, and multiple as are the demands. In *Code of the Street*, Anderson details the effects of these pressures in several compelling case studies, of men he calls John Turner and Roger Johnson.

In the chapter entitled "John Turner's Story," Anderson details the multiple pressures a young man faces as he attempts to broker his way between "street" and "decent" orientations. Anderson details Turner's arrest for gun possession, his problems on probation, his efforts to keep a job and care for his children, and his drug dealing. Turner was caught between various pressures. He writes, "On the streets a man like John might take a certain pride in having babies, in being good with his hands (able to fight), or even having jail time under his belt." However, these values don't necessarily translate well outside or beyond the street. He continues, "in terms of decent values such behavior is deemed irresponsible and even threatening" (p. 262). He sums up, "John envisioned a good life but was unable to accept the change in behavior necessary to achieve it. In fact, the street life competed quite effectively with his vision of the good life" (p. 289).

It is indeed a struggle to navigate one's way out of the "street" mindset, to become something of a role model for oneself and others. For Anderson, changing one's "outlook" is key in this regard. In the following chapter, "The Conversion of a Role Model: Looking for Mr. Johnson," Anderson talks about the tensions Roger Johnson has to endure as he leaves jail and tries to "turn his life around" by opening a small vending business. Anderson shows how Johnson must struggle with dominant society as he navigates his way around the "code of the street"—a code he embraced until recently. He is forced to comply with paperwork demands, with troublesome patrons, and so on, all the time trying to act "decent," all the time trying to be a good role model for younger people. Anderson writes, "It is by deftly interpreting and abiding by the rules of the code that [Johnson] is able to get through his days and nights, to manage the respect necessary to keep the drug dealers, scam artists and others at bay, or in line." Yet, this is not the only world Johnson must navigate: "At the same time he must function in the decent world as well, in the world of legitimate business practice—licenses, tax laws, and the like." He sums up, "The inner-city success story . . . requires the ability to code-switch, to play by the code of the street with the street element and the code of decency with others. Rob can do that, and in the process he works at setting an example for other young people" (1999, p. 310).

AUTHORITY AND DISCIPLINE

Anderson's position is compelling, allowing us to flesh out in greater detail some of the characteristics that such successful figures have. Yet such a focus should not occlude the perspective of youth themselves— what they're looking for, how they make sense out of such figures. Such a switch in perspective is rarely taken, though it takes us to the terrain of young people and authority—who has it, how it circulates, how it's validated, and why. I recall a conversation I had with Rufus and Tony early in 1997. I had planned on meeting Rufus and Tony at the club. Tony, however, had been grounded. I said I would come over if it was OK. He said it was. Much of our talk had to do with authority figures and respect. It was one of the first conversations we had before we both started working at the club.

Tony said, "If I see something wrong, I'ma let you know to your face—'I don't like you, you bogus, how you gonna do me?' Teachers for instance. They come in my face with an attitude. . . . [But] 'I ain't your child, you talk to me like you crazy, you talk to me like you some respect, some sense.' 'Pow, you outta here' [imitating teachers]. 'Pssss, so?' Then that really piss me off worser, 'cause you kick me out for telling you you wrong. They don't see my way. But that's pretty much why I'm at the alternative school now. Because, I, they say I got no respect for authority." He continued, "Just 'cause you got higher authority over us, don't let that go to your head. . . . I always tell people if you want my respect, you got to show me some respect." I asked if there were folks in authority positions either of them respected. Tony said, "It's not that many. 'Cause people, they let they authority get to their head." Rufus then added, "it seems like they scared of us teenagers nowadays . . . all they go by is the media and the press, that's all they going by." Tony concurred, "They use that authority to try to get over us . . . see if they really sit down and think about it, y'all think y'all little authority getting over us. Y'all ain't doing nothing but making us madder and we just gonna overcome y'all more." He continued, "It's not the authority. What makes everybody mad at school at these people is that they let that authority go to they head, pretty much, and they don't show no respect, but they expect you to respect them." Rufus summed up: "They abuse it."

I asked for an example of a bad authority figure. Tony said his old dean, who is black. His dean did the unforgivable, he told me, and called the police on him, thus deferring his authority.

> My dean, he black but everybody call him an Uncle Tom 'cause that's the way he treat everybody. . . . For one, he calls the police on a lot of black kids . . . situations that could be handled without the police. Like me and this kid, he stay in the neighborhood, he know both of us. All right, we gets to fighting, he call the police on us, when he knows he know both our parents personally and he can solve the situation with our parents. . . . Now we both got a record over something that you know could have been settled in the school with a suspension . . . be gone with it. Seem like since he knew I was on probation, he got me in all kinds of trouble. Nothing but trouble. Basically, that's why I'm back and forth in court, 'cause of him.

Indeed, both Rufus and Tony told me that they didn't respect people who handed problems over to others. They respected those who settled them face-to-face. Tony commented approvingly on one of his teachers from high school.

> Miss Jackson, the teacher, she don't play, she gonna come, she straight about her business, all right. She did like this, this exactly what she said, she said, "OK, all right, yeah, I might look like I'm mean, but I'm not mean, I'm real nice. . . . I don't like to kick kids out my class unless I really, really have to," she says, "but if you feel like you got something against me, you wanna fight me,

tell me, 'cause if I got something against you, I'm gonna tell you
to your face, if you bad enough to hit me, then hit me, 'cause I
ain't running to the principal like all these other teachers. I'm
gonna hit you back and I guarantee you gonna hit the floor." She
crazy, but I always respected that.

Importantly for Tony, Miss Jackson would not hand her authority over to
the principal. She handled it by herself.

While the example of Miss Jackson was an aggressive, physical
one—made all the more interesting given that she's a woman—much of
their talk also had to do with the fine balance between authority and care.
I asked if there were other people they respected, that they listen to. Tony
mentioned his granddad. He said, "You do wrong, he won't come at you
in a negative way, trying to punish you and everything. He'll just tell you
right from wrong. All he says, 'I can't do nothing to you, all I can do is
try to lead you in the right way.' That's why I always respect my grandfather." He also mentioned, of course, Johnny. Like his granddad, Johnny
was not simply a disciplinarian. While he could be authoritative, this was
rooted in a profound sense of caring, and also mutual respect. It was a
highly fraught balance. At one point, Tony, still in his gang, said,

That's why Johnny got my respect. And then he seen me, 'cause,
you know, I ain't gonna lie, I'm in a gang and everything, you
know what I'm saying? And he seen me doing my little gang stuff
and everything in the club and then he'll come and sit down and
talk to me about instead of putting me out. 'Cause he know where
I come from, he know why I done been through, through all my
life. He know my daddy, he know my mamma . . . he know my
whole family, put it like that, both sides. So he know where I'm
coming from. He know my dad wasn't around. . . . He sat down,
he talked to me, tell me I can't let my dad get involved in all my
decisions, put everything off on my dad. And then when I sit
down and think about it all that, I'm like Johnny, right. . . . Don't
disrespect my mom for something he [his dad] be doin' in my
life. Johnny done played a very positive role in my life. That's
why I always show John respect. If he catch me doing some
things that disrespect him in his face, I always go back to him and

I'm like, "Johnny, yo man, I'm sorry for what I did. Is there anything you need me to do to make up for it, just let me know."
That's why I basically I do volunteer service at the club a lot now.

Johnny's relationship to both teens was intense. As Tony noted above,
Johnny has known him his whole life, knew both sides of his family. He
was able to give advice to Tony from a vantage point that made sense to
him. His relationship with Johnny led to Tony volunteering at the club and
also, as noted, a staff position. Tony could relate to Johnny, which made
all the difference. Indeed, when Tony said the above, Rufus responded,
"He probably been through the same thing." He said, as well, "That's how
open Johnny gets, like, he'll tell you anything about his life. If you ask him
a question, you know, he's just open about himself, period."

JOHNNY

It would be impossible to overstate Johnny's importance in Rufus and
Tony's lives. He was, in many respects, a benchmark figure for these
young men, one who all but embodied what a successful transition to
adulthood might mean. The following was prepared by Tony—with
Rufus's help—as a tribute to Johnny. Written in 1998, after Tony and
Rufus's experiences as staff members at the club, it summed up much:

Johnny is the man who never gives up. I been knowing him since
I was three years old. He has been like a father to me. He has
been there to discipline, guide, and council me. I got into a little
trouble when I was younger and I didn't want to tell DD [another
staff member] or Johnny because I didn't want to let them down.
But Lord knows, you can't hide anything from Johnny! It seemed
like every time I got into trouble, he would get mad but I could
talk to him. The club is a second home to me and Johnny is like
the father. He is always there to explain things to me and help
guide me. Negative influences in the community, when they get
around Johnny's building, there is nothing but respect. He never
let me bring negativity into the club. Based on my experience of
negativity in the community, I know firsthand when you walk in
the door, it stops. With Johnny's support and counsel, I got out of

the gang. I left my bad ways behind. But as negative as I was, I never gave up on school, which Johnny always stressed—education comes first. I never failed a grade. I got two jobs now. He was there to stay on my back about a job. In the future, I want to become either a teacher or a lawyer—that way I can help other people the way Johnny helped me. I want to be there to council people, break it down, and lead my life in the direction Johnny led his. People say that Martin Luther King or Abraham Lincoln or George Washington are their heroes. In my mind, Johnny is the famous person in my life who's a hero.

As evidenced by this text, Johnny had several qualities Tony and Rufus gravitated towards and resonated with.

Tony stressed that Johnny was like a father to him. While neither Rufus nor Tony's fathers were much in the picture, Johnny had always been their for both of them, giving himself over to them and the community in selfless ways. As both Rufus and Tony observed, Johnny made an extraordinary amount of money by community standards. However, he maintained his home in the neighborhood as well as all of his old allegiances and friendship networks. Tony noted:

He got all this money, but he wish to fix him up a fancy house in the middle of the ghetto, you know what I'm saying? That's what I really like about Johnny, 'cause he ain't trying, 'cause like most black people . . . when they get the money to they head, they try to get away and get the biggest fanciest house, the fanciest cars.

"Moving up," thus, was not equated with "moving out" for Johnny. While many equate success with rupturing old ties (i.e., as Tony put it, "saying they don't want to live the way they used to"), Johnny, in explicit contrast, has stuck with the neighborhood and his friends, implying values of selflessness and community. His love for them both, it seemed, was unconditional: "Johnny is the man who never gives up." As Rufus said, "Everybody just depend on Johnny."

Johnny was also able to serve a protective role for both teens. No matter who was out to get you, it stopped when you walked through the door to the club. It was a protected space, made so largely through the respect Johnny generated in the community. Johnny, as unit director of the club, had to settle many conflicts and fights between teens. A physically imposing man who lifted weights at the club with many of the youth, Johnny was not averse to physically intervening between combatants; indeed, he marked this as a source of pride. Johnny worked hard to earn the respect of younger club members, and a large part of that was his physical presence. He was highly respected by many young people in town, including many gang members and leaders who tended to keep their conflicts away from the club at his behest. However, more important than his physical prowess was his ability to settle conflicts without fighting. When Johnny, after nearly 2 decades, retired, he was replaced by a younger man, a former football player who weighed over 300 pounds. Johnny commented to me that his size would not necessarily help him with trouble-making teens. Maintaining control was largely a mental endeavor, effected by way of roots in the community as well as by the ability to generate a more intangible kind of respect. This protection was rooted firmly in an ethic of care—one that extended into all areas of their lives.

Johnny embodies for both young people what John Devine might call a "caring panopticon," or mode of surveillance. Indeed, Johnny used information about young people in very strategic ways, always letting young people know that he is aware of everything that was happening, that he always had an eye on them—as Tony noted above, "Lord knows you can't hide anything from Johnny!" John Devine (1995) argued in *Maximum Security* that educative figures should strive to keep a kind of "surveillance" over students, as part of the more broadly humanistic goal of engaging the whole student—not just the disembodied mind. Students have complex lives and educators should strive to meet them there in all of their complexity if they are to be successful. Surveillance, in and of itself, is not bad, according to Devine—it is a question of towards what end it is mobilized. This kind of surveillance over young people took place inside as well as outside of the club. Johnny mobilized information in subtle and not-so-subtle ways to let young people know that their actions were always monitored, to prevent them from key transgressions, which often had life-and-death consequences—as in, for example, the decision to join a gang.

Johnny's history in the community, his links with families in this tightly knit town, allowed him to engage in such practices in ways others could not. In fact, Johnny grew up with—and often raised, as he put it—many of their parents. He was thus, as he was fond of pointing out, a conduit for information—from every corner of the neighborhood to their guardians. I recall driving though Hub City with Johnny, as he spotted a young girl hanging on the street corner with some boys. "I'm gonna tell her mama!" he said. These are, it is important to note, locally validated kinds of authority. Johnny would never, for example, call the police on a young person (as did Tony's dean), nor would he ever "inform" on anyone. He was a kind of protective force to them all, in a neighborhood cross-cut by many different kinds of dangers.

Finally, Johnny was an important cultural broker. He provided guidance that made sense to these young men. During the talk referenced above, when we coproduced Tony's essay about Johnny, both pointed out how Johnny is able to "break down" things in a way that makes sense to them—whether it's school, their social lives, work, or any of the institutions with which they were involved. During this discussion, Rufus commented that Johnny could take a complex business idea and be able to sell it to elite, "powerful people" in a way they would be able to understand. Johnny could then turn around, Rufus said, and "break it down" for people like himself and say "OK, this is what it's really all about." Johnny was a constant source of tips and advice about a range of things—from romance to jobs to education. He was also a source of connections. For example, if court ordered, both said that Johnny always had community service work available. He could also speak to probation officers, members of the court, and so on. Johnny knew "everyone," from powerful businesspeople to politicians to gang leaders. He encouraged young people to do the same, to embrace local values in ways that do not put success and identity at cross-purposes with each other. Rufus said,

> Me and Johnny, we know the hardest dudes in Hub City, hardest dudes, I mean, we know killers drug dealers, everything. They come to the club, they got a whole different face. I mean, the hardest people. You give me prisoners. . . . I betcha Johnny know him, they come in there, they [in a soft voice] "What's up John, how you doing?" . . . They in there playing pool with kids, "Come on young boy, let's play fussball, I betcha I can whoop you."

Rufus went on to say that Johnny's influence extended "upward" so to speak, as well. "Then he got mayors, doctors, he got lawyers, he got people that got their own businesses, they come to the club, 'What's up John, how you doing?' They got they suits on, they beepers, they phone ringing. But they ain't trying to hear that, they talking to Johnny . . . they at the club." Johnny was key for both as they began to fashion "possible selves"—selves that could generate respect from different kinds of people for different reasons. As Tony said, "I want to be there to council people, break it down, and lead my life in the direction Johnny led his."

This self fashioning was complex. It was not simply imitative. In fact, Johnny often said that it was impossible to "imitate" him. Johnny has been a caring and validated part of the community and the club for nearly his entire life. As he stated many times, again, he grew up with and even "raised" many of the children's parents. He was someone to whom many young people looked for guidance, social capital, and perhaps most importantly, protection. At one point during the particularly stressful summer, discussed in the last chapter, several new staff people, myself included, were criticized for yelling too often and being overly strict. Johnny, who has a fierce reputation as a disciplinarian, said the only reason he can be this strict is that young people see him "in a protective role." This again was tied up in his own biography, his own longstanding role in the community.

As noted, the middle-class model of development—where generational distinctions are clearly marked, where one simply moved from and between youth to adulthood—is not wholly relevant here. These youth could not "fashion selves" by separating themselves from the community. In fact, they looked up to Johnny precisely because he did not do this. Importantly, both Rufus and Tony saw part of "growing up" as an explicit obligation to be there for others—for those younger, for peers, for those older. I recall a paper Tony wrote for class. In it, he said that if he had a million dollars, he would give 50% to the community, 25% to his mother, and keep 25% for himself. These young people lived their lives in the "in between," in between various pressures and demands. To evoke Alex Kotlowitz once again, "There are no children here."

It is critical, following the above, to focus on the ideal characteristics of role models such as Johnny. But our discussion should not end there. It seems to me that we need to focus on young people as active agents in this process, acknowledging the work they do navigating their way towards adulthood. We need to move, I think, closer and closer to young people's lives in all their complexity—including their relationships with each other and with those younger. We must situate these young men's relationships with those older within an expansive context, one that accounts for multiple relationships in and across multiple institutions. I would like to focus now, in contrast with much of the sociological work on old heads, on the work of young people themselves in this process of self-definition. At best, it seems, we see these figures help young people articulate their social networks in new, more positive directions. Football—so encouraged by Johnny—was one place where this happened.

FOOTBALL

I got a call from Rufus a week or so after the club opened, asking if I could drive him to football the next morning. Games began at 9:00 a.m. Players had to be there after 8:00. Through I worked Friday nights at the club and, by night, was exhausted, I said I would be there. I was a "for-sure ride" to football. Reciprocity is key to all relationships, of course. As I noted earlier, as time went on, Rufus and Tony became bigger and bigger parts of my study. I made demands on their time, for interviews, to hang out, and so on. As time went on, they began to make demands on me as well. This meant trips to the Laundromat and shopping out of town, among other things. This was largely how I was useful in their lives.

Rufus lived on the bottom floor of a house, located a few blocks from the club. It was early and the streets were mostly empty—no kids out in the street, no steady stream of cars. I waited for a few minutes out in front in my car for our 8:00 a.m. rendezvous. Rufus was usually late, but I hesitated ringing the bell. Mary was ill and spent lots of time in bed. I didn't want to wake her up. Rufus came to the door a few minutes later. He had just gotten off the phone with Tony. It was the first game of the season. Tony said he would be there. Rufus got in the car—football gear and all—and we drove over to Tony's house.

When we got there, however, Tony said he wouldn't be driving with us after all. He was going to wait for his cousin Joe to come by. Joe had a car but didn't know how to get to the field. He wanted to be there, too. Tony brought out a CD and said he wanted Rufus to listen to it on the way "for inspiration." It was "Rapper's Ball" by rapper E-40. He grabbed his head when giving him the CD and said, "I better see you hurt somebody!" He had on his McDonald's T-shirt. He was going to go to work right after the game.

We got to the field at about 8:30—before spectators came to watch and after parents dropped off their children and went back home. I was alone for about a half-hour. The players all changed in what they called "the club house" before coming out onto the field. An older black man showed up soon after and sat right in front of me. He was there to watch one of his children play. Conversation turned rather quickly to questions of discipline, of what it takes to stay "on the right track" in life. He told me that another one of his kids had gotten a scholarship to a local state school, "but she partied and threw it away." He told me, however, that his kids were well behaved. "I beat 'em," he said matter-of-factly.

The game began promptly at 9:00. Tony and Joe showed up a little after it started. Tony spotted me and walked over to where I was sitting in the stands. Joe walked over to the fence where the game was being played. Tony scanned the field, looking for Rufus. When he spotted him, he called out "Seventy-six! Seventy-six!," his number. The stands were beginning to fill up. Tony soon got up and joined Joe and others by the side of the fence. Tony's demeanor changed quickly. Becoming animated and aggressive, he called out to someone on their other team, "Look at them legs! They look like pegs! You walking on air! You ain't nothing!" His jeering was not reserved for Rufus's opponents, however. He called out to another player on the sidelines, "I'm getting more time than you!"

Clearly, he wanted to be in the game. Tony was at an alternative high school that did not have a sports team. He had joined the club's basketball team but only lasted a game or two. That didn't stop him from offering advice, however—advice about the game, how everyone was playing, what kind of plays they should run, and so forth. He got more and more excited as the game went on. At one point, he said, "I want to play so bad!" and then said, "uuuhhh," mimicking rapper Master P's famous catchphrase. "I'm gonna show them how Mississippi boys play!" and then, "That coach is snapping! That's a Mississippi coach!" Rufus's team lost, however. After the game, they all took off in Joe's car, Rufus back home, and Tony to McDonald's for a long day and night of work.

I drove Rufus to nearly all of his home football games that fall. I was, to use his mother's phrase, his "for-sure ride." The next week, I came by his place a little before 8:00. He was talking outside his house with another teenager on the team, Victor, and Victor's mom. While Victor's mom said she would be happy to drive, Rufus said "Greg'll give me a ride." He got in the car and looked over the CDs I had, choosing a compilation CD called *Southwest Riders* that featured artists from the South, West Coast, and Midwest, such as 666 Mafia and Eightball and MJG. He chose the track "Threesixafix" by 666 Mafia and played it again and again. Victor had arrived by the time we got there, along with another neighborhood youth, Shaun. Right before the game, Victor joined Rufus in my car, and we played "Threesixafix" several times. They needed to "psych themselves up," they said, laughing and cheering at lines like "Smoke your ass like a black and mild [a popular cigar]!"

They won the game. Afterwards, a number of young people crowded around me, looking for rides back home. Some, like Shaun, I knew. Others, like Oscar, I didn't. Oscar came out of the clubhouse in green fatigues, his hat on, cocked in the style of local gangs, clearly happy about the win. Oscar was in a gang—when he said "hi" to me, he cocked his fingers as if tossing up a gang sign. We crowded in my car and took off. The *Southwest Riders* CD was still on and Oscar began rapping off it, substituting intricate gang-related imagery—that of putting "down" sixes and "up" fives—for song lyrics. Oscar was affiliated with a five-point gang and like lots of young people in gangs, could create elaborate raps using gang symbolism, inserting it into all kinds of other texts.

As I pulled up Oscar's block to drop him off I saw several older men right in front of his house. They were hanging out, with their hats cocked to the side, beers in hands, sitting on motorbikes. They were blocking traffic with their bikes, effectively claiming the street. Rap music played loudly out of a box radio. When they recognized that Oscar was in my car, they let me pass, though they looked at me with hard, deadened eyes. While I knew many young people in gangs, these men were slightly older and seemed far more entrenched to me, more "hard core." Afterward, Rufus said that it was good that Oscar was coming out for football. It might be a good way to mitigate against all the negative influences that surrounded him. He had worked to get Tony out of his gang, he told me, and was now going to do the same for Oscar.

The desire to help others was key here. Just as Johnny and others helped him, Rufus tried to help others. Indeed, midway through that season, Rufus asked me if we could take someone else to practice—a 10-

year-old boy named Gary who lived down the block. Gary wound up coming with us for the next few weeks. He was quiet, mostly keeping to himself. Interestingly, Rufus called him "young blood" several times, and said he reminded him of himself when he was younger. He even encouraged Gary to come to the club. I recall Rufus one night wrestling with Gary outside the club, after it closed. A parent drove by and was alarmed. Johnny said, "its not like that, they're cousins."

The following week, Rufus would be traveling with the team for an away game. But Tony called me early that morning, asking if I would drive him out. I said I would. I picked him up a little after 9:00. The night before at McDonald's had been taxing, he said. He told me that one of his "enemies" had come there the night before, looking for him. However, he said that he had a lot of support in town, that his manager wanted to call the police: "I had the whole crew there! I told them, 'You know where I live, where I work. I got two guns—my fists.'" Much of this, of course, was bravado. Tony was trying to get himself out of the gang, but there were these pressures—from his own gang members and from others. In fact, there had been a shooting the night before and Tony was afraid that people might think he was still affiliated with a gang, might come after him. Yet, he stressed one immutable truth—you needed friends to watch your back.

This came up the following week, as well, as I drove Rufus, Tony, and Oscar back home after a game. As we drove up one of the main city streets, we passed a member of Tony's old gang, Chuck. Chuck was walking past a local restaurant, not too far from the club. We all waved "hi." Earlier, Tony told us, he had run into Chuck, who asked him where he was, if he was still in the gang. "We miss you!" he said.

Oscar, who was sitting in the backseat, seemed momentarily puzzled. He then asked Tony, "So who you with now?" to which Tony responded, "I'm not with nobody." Rufus added quickly, "We don't need to be with anybody. Nobody messes with us." Oscar responded, almost in defeat, "I need my guys to fight." Tony said that he, Rufus, and Joe were going to form "The Nitro Clique"—that he trusted them before anybody, that they were like a gang. This distinction between cliques and gangs, as noted in Chapter 2, was an important one, allowing Rufus and Tony to distance their friendship (and the support it implied) from the negative connotations of gangs.

While many of Rufus's cousins came out for his games, his mother Mary was noticeably absent for most of the season. Mary had said she would come a few times in previous weeks. But she never quite made it. She was always tired, always felt overwhelmed. For the last game of the season that November, however, she would be there. It was difficult for Mary to get out of the house. I agreed to drive Rufus earlier in the day, before returning for Mary and, it turned out, her friend Leroy. When I got her, she gave me a card, saying "That's your boy!" It was a mock football card with Rufus's picture, which she had bought from his school. I sat with Mary and Leroy for the game. "That's my baby! Go baby!" she called out again and again. Leroy was more stoic, commenting tersely on the coach, the plays, and so on.

Mary and Rufus's relationship was complicated, different in most ways from the traditional, hierarchical parent/child dyad. She had a hard time disciplining him, for example. Indeed, she told me that afternoon that she had no one but Johnny to call when Rufus misbehaved. Rufus's father was long out of the picture and Johnny was the only one she could call on. Even when she got his report card, she said, she could not quite decode it, could not quite tell if it was good or bad. She said she was glad that Rufus was working at the club. But she was also afraid that too much of his time would be taken up there. She was conflicted, not sure what kind of advice to give him, how to support him. In fact, we spent much of the game talking about how Rufus had gotten in trouble a few weeks earlier, throwing stones at a bus. Rufus had been with two of his cousins, Joe and Tommy, who had gotten into worse trouble. In fact, because Joe had a police record already, she said, he admitted to throwing most of the stones, taking much of the blame. She understood the bonds between Rufus and his cousins—in fact, her best friend growing up in Humbrick was Tony's aunt Gloria, Rufus's godmother—but still feared they would get him in trouble. This was a key tension, one through which she felt somewhat ill-equipped to guide him. She was glad Johnny was there to help her.

In closing, several complex webs of authority emerge here, between and across generations. There is Rufus looking to Johnny for guidance, while trying to be there for his "young blood" Gary. There is also Mary trying to be there for Rufus while looking to Johnny for advice. Finally, there is Tony and his cousins endeavoring to support Rufus throughout the season, as they strive to channel their modes of association into something more positive. Authority here isn't simply the young deferring to or imitating the old. Rather, authority is realized and validated in the particular demands of situations and is always rooted in a profound sense of care for others in the community.

TWO KEY COMMUNITY-BASED PROGRAMS

In what follows, I highlight two other key programs these young men gravitated towards as they struggled towards adulthood. In each case, these programs allowed these young men to take on coveted authority roles in activities rooted in, and validated by, the local community. This is key. Young black men often have few ways in which they can act in validated positions of authority. Like the junior staff positions at the community center, these were important (though less formal) positions, rooted in the local community and its imperatives. They provided key opportunities for young men to model themselves, in authentic ways, on positive older figures. This didn't mean, however, the kind of uncritical deference to older figures often privileged in school. It meant increased connections to the community, including those younger.

Egyptian Lodge

During early 1998, after the end of the football season, both Rufus and Tony as well as several other young men from the neighborhood joined what was essentially a "Junior Egyptian Lodge" club, sponsored by the so-called Egyptian Lodge in town. The Egyptian Lodge was a local club made up of older black men who met in a converted store front. The Junior Lodge was a program they sponsored for younger black men to give them "positive" kinds of activities. The attraction was multifaceted, but due in large part to the influence of an older staff person, Doug, who was an Egyptian Lodge member and had longstanding ties in the community. Like Johnny, Doug knew all the youth in the neighborhood and their families. Indeed, Doug often told young people, "I know your mama!" or would ask, "Who are you kin to?" when chastising young people. The implication was clear—his influence extended beyond the club walls, into the community.

Doug was in his early 20s. Not quite an elder like Johnny, not quite a young person, Doug was able to function as a kind of informal pedagogue for many of the teens, who looked up to him. Like Johnny, he was totally committed to youth in the neighborhood. In fact, Doug left a job at a large food company in 1997 to follow his self-professed dream of working with young people. Other staff members and children alike often noted that his taking this job at the center (which paid about $6 an hour) meant taking a very serous pay cut, indicating his high degree of commitment. Lots of the teens knew where he lived in town and often came by his house to hang out and to chat. Doug ran the gym. He soon became "teen coordinator"—a role that suited him particularly well.

I recall one night in 1998. The club was closing early and Doug, Johnny, and I were hanging out in the hallway, with about five young people who were waiting to be picked up. One girl asked Doug if he knew her mother. He said he did, she was a "distant cousin, not by blood" and he only met her once. The girl was excited—Doug seemed to know everyone. "This is a small town," he said. "Everyone knows everyone." Talk soon turned to a local bar where two large, local families had had a fight. The two families were well known. Lots of them and their kin had come to the club over the years. A little later, an older woman came by to pick up her grandson. She had known Johnny and Doug for years. She sat down. There were still a few kids left playing in the club and their parents were late picking them up. "Parents forget their kids," Doug said. "When I was younger the club was stricter." A passing janitor said, "Any other place, they would call DCFS [Department of Children and Family Services]." This was not an option, of course. Johnny said that they were "doing well occupying themselves." Doug replied, "They've had practice, you know what I mean."

Doug spent lots of time, after the club was closed, talking to teens. I recall another conversation one night. This evening, we talked about religion, the Egyptian Lodge, and the community in general. Doug said that there were "too many divisions between people" and "organizations splinter off into different ones," often fighting one another. This was true of gangs as well as of churches. There are "forty-five black churches in Hub City," Doug said. "Every time there's five people, they want to start a church." The Egyptian Lodge, in contrast, was a black-based organization, not rooted in politics or in religion. Of course, the Egyptian Lodge were not a gang, either, though they thrived on much of the same sense of secrecy and insider knowledge. I had the sense, talking to Rufus, Tony, and several other of the teens, that the group provided an ideology that made sense to them. Much of the attraction for these teens was wrapped up in a kind of popular hybrid of Afrocentrism and black nationalism. For example, that night Doug discussed a book he read, which talked about how melanin was magnetic, giving black people special energy from the sun. There was also some talk about how Napoleon shot the nose of the Sphinx in Egypt so it would not appear African. At one point, Rufus said he was "confused about what to study," that he felt society was coming down hard on him about what he was or should be. He said he didn't know whether to "go to the streets" or to "study on black history." He felt less confused with time, especially though his involvement with the Egyptian Lodge.

These were complex issues, reflecting the often very mixed sets of messages and imperatives these youth face. Rufus said that he wished he could skip high school and go straight to college. He didn't want only to take tests, but to write papers, to be self-motivated. Doug concurred. He was only a few credits away from his associate's degree himself. Doug said that white kids often have very little to think about or worry about. They can do well in school because it's all they have to worry about. He understood, from experience, that kids growing up in Hub City don't always have that luxury. Also, he said, "School doesn't measure street smarts"—the kind of smarts they all shared. He then looked at a young person who had a reputation for selling drugs and said, "It's not just being 'bout it' [a phrase used by popular "gangsta" rapper Master P]. I'm not talking about hustling or selling drugs!" Doug had a lot of family in local gangs—he knew what he was talking about. He then said, "I'm talking about survival—like Master P said, how to make a dollar out of fifteen cents." Like Johnny, Doug's power was highly personal, not positional. He understood where these young men were coming from. He was able to attract a whole "clique" of youth to the club and then to the lodge.

The group also gave neighborhood youth the opportunity to do things like throw parties. This was very important. From the very first conversations I had with Rufus and Tony, the idea of organizing and throwing parties for the community was on their minds, as a way to bring some unity to the neighborhood and avoid incipient gang conflicts. Many of the areas where folks used to congregate, they said, had closed down—

all except for the lodge. Discussing the neighborhood, Tony said "31st Street done died down. The only thing that's keeping it alive is the Lodge. . . . Friends [a neighborhood bar], they done went out of business. . . . So now they renting it out for parties. . . . We gonna have my auntie talk to the dude, and we gonna rent it for Fridays and Saturdays." Rufus added, "Right now it's just trying to get the money." These parties would be places where gang conflicts would be left behind. Rufus said, "You can't come in there with no ana [animosity]. I don't care if you Folks or you Stone, you in a gang, you not in a gang, don't come in there." He added, "We understand you wanna be hard but this is . . . a truce area . . . we coming in here to party, have a good time." This seemed well within reach: "All we gotta do really is throw a stereo set, get some old chairs . . . few tables and stuff." Importantly, this could be passed on to those younger. "You got peers doing it and then once we get so old, we can pass it on to the teenagers. That way it's just constantly going."

The desire to organize and throw parties for the community became a reality though their involvement with the Junior Egyptian Lodge. The group gave them lodge space to do this, though they had to come up with ways to advertise their shows, as well as get a DJ. Planning was complex, and the task fell to the young men. I remember one night in particular, I got a call from Tony at 7:00 p.m. He asked me if I had a computer and could I let them use it to make up a flyer for a Lodge party that Friday. "Of course," I said, "sure." Soon, Tony and Rufus as well as two other youth were at my apartment. We booted up the computer, loaded Word, and got to work. One of the youth first typed "Party" at the top of the page and then wrote, "once again we bring it to you." Rufus suggested "bringing it to you" but the rest said that was too "ghetto"—too "low class." He then typed "for the players" but others said they wanted to invite "player haters" too and also "females." He then typed "no refreshments, drugs, or passes out." Tony said he didn't want people coming in and out. We then had a fairly heated discussion about putting "donations" or "fee" on the flyer. Rufus said it was a fund-raiser so they would have to put "donation." Tony said that if they put "donation," there would be too many "ghetto-type people" who would think they could come for free. We settled on the former before driving over to an all-night copy store and making copies. As we drove up a main street, we passed some white kids. Tony reached out of the car to give them a flyer. "We're multicultural!"

he said. These parties were key for these young men, a place where their social networks could flourish, outside the gang context in new ways.

Teen Center

When Johnny retired from the center in early 1998, he was replaced by a younger man, someone who might be able to help attract teenagers to the club. Traditionally, clubs like this one would either attract older teens or younger children. This particular center tended to attract the latter. The upper administration, with the help of some large grants, wanted to perhaps change this, and see if we could strike a more equitable balance. This meant encouraging a whole constellation of activities, a "teen center" among them. Because the weekly discussion groups I was conducting were deemed helpful, and I generally attracted older teenagers as well as younger people, I was asked to take part in some of the initial planning meetings with teens. I was also asked, eventually, to turn my weekly meetings on music into a "teen club" activity that would allow us to do activities at the club and in the community.

We had several meetings that spring about these new initiatives and also about the center. At the first meeting, the new director, Henry, stressed how he wanted to give teens more freedom than they traditionally had at the club—freedom to set their own agenda and manage their own space. He made a point of saying that he liked rap music, subscribed to *The Source*, a popular rap magazine, and also liked Play Station. The first thing he did was designate a small, glass-encased "teen center," exclusively for teens. While this space had always been reserved for teens, when there were few teens present the room had often been used for other activities. Henry said he would only allow teens in the room; even when the club was full and no one was in it, it would still only be a teen center. Among other things, he bought a VCR, a stereo, and a game system for the room. We also agreed to elect a group of "officers" who could discuss potential problems as they came up—positions that Rufus and Tony, among others, took over.

As noted earlier, Rufus and Tony faced multiple demands as they struggled their way toward adulthood, as they tried to be good models for those younger than them. In particular, Tony felt an imperative to be there for others as Johnny (among others) had been there for him. Though the teen center, Tony was adamant about starting a mentoring program, with personalized tutoring, talks, and also trips. We wound up doing two trips, going bowling and also roller skating together. In fact, Tony made a point of saying that he wanted his mentoring "partner" or "mentee" to be a young man in the community who had had some problems, had been involved in some gang activity in Chicago from a very young age. He told this young man during one of our meetings:

> Pretty much, you ain't seen it till I seen it like I seen it, living that life, that hard-core life, it ain't nothing man but trouble man. The hard core got me on probation since ninety-three. Hard-core life got me put in jail. I look at that hard-core life now that I just beat a seven-year term. The judge told me the next time I get in some trouble, he sending me to prison. Not no kiddy prison, adult prison. . . . Not the county prison, I mean prison prison, ball and chain prison. Judge told me, if I get in any more trouble, that's where he gonna send me. So I look at this, man this a wake up call for me. Ain't time to play no more. It's time to get serious and wake up, get a job, keep a job, get out there, try to find you a place to stay, take care of responsibilities like an adult. 'Cause now, once you turn seventeen, they gonna treat you in the judicial system [like] an adult. So you gotta treat your life like you an adult, run your life right. 'Cause your mama, she ain't gonna come and get you, every time you get in trouble. She ain't gonna have no $101 dollars [bail] to come and get you outta county or however much it costs to get you out. It ain't no joke. Boy, I'm telling you man, straighten your life up, you living the wrong life, you running the streets at a young age, man, or you trying to be hard, trying to live your life rough. Better straighten it up now . . . 'cause if you don't, it's gonna happen when it too late. Then you gonna be, like, "I shoulda listened to them fellas right there when they told me." 'Cause I know I sure regret it. I messed up my whole youth life, my whole teen life.

It was critical for Tony to serve this role for younger people and he saw the club and its activities as intrinsic to this. He saw this, in part, as the charge that Johnny laid out for him—the imperative to be a role model, to give direction to those younger. Recall his comment from his text about Johnny: "I want to be there to council people, break it down, and lead my life in the direction Johnny led his." In fact, Tony and I often discussed how people who could speak from experience about life's hardships and temptations were so important for those younger than them. Tony desperately wanted to be one of these figures.

The summer came to an end with a renewed resolution to attract more teens to the club. In fact, Tony stopped working as staff at this time, in an effort to spend more time developing teen activities. He was beginning to attract the kind of positive attention that Rufus had attracted earlier. He told me, early that September, that a reporter had been by and interviewed him about the club. They were going to do an article, about the club entitled "Not Just For Kids Anymore." Apparently one of the staff members had told the reporter that Tony was an active club member "trying to turn his life around." He told the reporter that he didn't want to see "kids going through what he went through."

In addition, Tony was getting an award from a local sorority—an award that recognized how greatly he turned his life around—during a "Pride Day" event at a local park. Held yearly, different groups and businesses from the community would set up tables for this daylong event. The club always had a table and several of the teens would be volunteering at it. Tony seemed very happy about all this and said a number of good things were happening this week. He said he hoped the article on him had come out by the time pride day rolled around. The event, held the following week, was exciting. There were various booths set up, and also a stage. The club had a booth, stocked with pictures of the club and some literature. Henry and Doug were there, signing up kids and parents for yearlong memberships. At one point, a dance group from Chicago took the stage. In beautiful, syncopated style, they step-danced off a song by popular R&B artist Allyah, using their stomping feet as percussion.

Before long, I ran into a young person I knew from a few years earlier. He had attended the club when I first started conducting discussion groups. He was now in a gang. I asked him how he was doing. He quietly said OK. He asked if I was still at the club. I said I was. I then told him about some of the teen programs. A few more young people in this gang soon came over, all greeting each other with the complex five-point shake. An older group of men stood a few feet away, doing the six-point shake of a rival gang. As this was going on, I spotted some of the teens from the club, congregating together, just like the young gang members nearby. The parallels were striking. Towards the end of the day, Tony received his award. The presenter stressed that Tony was a "good role model," both for those younger and also—just as importantly—for his peers.

FINAL THOUGHTS

Under the guidance of validated, older members of the community, Rufus and Tony and their friends engaged in different kinds of activities that gave them alternatives to "the street." These social networks were critical modes of support necessary for everyday survival. Yet these networks existed in a context where they were often "criminalized" and where they often exerted demands in equal measure. For these young men, this transition towards adulthood has been a struggle—a struggle to be there for younger people, to look for guidance from those older—cross-cut by the real and perceived immediacies and dangers of social support systems.

I remember one night early in the fall of 1998. I was writing up the data from my original study while volunteering at the club. The Teen Center was up and running, attracting a steady if small group of youth. At one point, a scuffle broke out in the center. Two youth emerged, clearly angry. One youth, involved in the Junior Egyptian Lodge, said, "Keep your hands off my brother!" The other responded, "I don't care if you're Larry Hoover [imprisoned head of the Gangster Disciples]! What are you going to do!" By aggressively referring to his fellow Junior Egyptian Lodge member as a "brother," this first youth was evoking fierce, gang-like allegiances. By referencing Larry Hoover, the second youth acknowledged this, while challenging it. Doug said immediately, "That's not what the group is about!"

The interaction seemed relatively innocuous at the time. However, as I noted in Chapter 1, the allegiances between these teens could be rearticulated in very dangerous ways, very quickly. They existed in and within a local social context which made them vulnerable to many different kinds of dangers. These dangers always loomed, always threatened the paths these young men laid out, always threatened my ability to tell a simple story. I turn now—always the "vulnerable observer"—to this story's conclusion (Behar, 1996).

CHAPTER FIVE

Struggling Towards Success: Today and Tomorrow

Throughout this book, I have struggled to tell a different kind of story about young black men, a story that looks beyond neat narratives about "good" and "bad" youth and their social and institutional pathways towards "success" and "failure." Understanding Rufus and Tony's lives in new ways demanded, as noted, that I bracket my initial research agenda on popular culture and education. It demanded, instead, that I navigate a terrain with no safe shores, without the "steadfast truths, and monolithic ways of imagining the relation between self and community" that often gird the research process (Behar, 1996, p. 32). Opening myself up in this way—becoming the "vulnerable observer" Ruth Behar writes about—meant getting closer to the everyday lives of these young people. In particular, it meant understanding how quickly and how totally their lives could be derailed by large and small real-world contingencies.

In this chapter, I return to the moment I highlighted in the opening chapter, the moment these young men met in the hospital. I trace their lives over the following few months, highlighting the fragility of the circumstances in which they found themselves. I use this discussion to situate the chapter's final section, a series of recent reflections on what it meant—and what it still means—to "grow up" or "become men" in this dangerous and unpredictable terrain. I try to give the reader, here, a better way to understand what "success" means in the lives of these young men. Such a discussion will allow us to understand in sharper and more nuanced ways the importance of—and the stakes involved in—meeting young people "where they're at" today.

1998–1999: STRUGGLE AND TRANSITION

By late October 1998, I was volunteering regularly at the club, working at the front desk, trying to coordinate activities with the new teen center at the club. I saw Tony and Rufus frequently as well—perhaps more than any other of my friends or family members. Earlier, I had taken Rufus to the supermarket, where he ran into one of his old teachers. He told her about his mom, how she was back in the hospital yet again. Mary, recall, had gained 30 pounds in one month—the result, we found out, of kidney failure. The teacher remembered Rufus fondly. "Bless your heart," she said—she knew how devoted he was to his mother and her well-being. Rufus picked up a number of job applications that day. Mary's medical bills were rising and he needed to think about bringing in a steady income. I dropped Rufus back at the hospital later that afternoon, before taking Tony shopping at the Dollar General. He needed, he told me, to pick up some snacks "for the kids" back home. As I said earlier, I was at the writing stage of my ethnographic endeavors at this point, giving shape and coherence to the lives of the young people with whom I worked weekly, while becoming more and more immersed in the lives of Rufus and Tony. Indeed, many of my days were like this one—filled up with the immediate pressures and demands of their everyday needs.

Later that week, the third week in October, I went to work the front desk at the club. As per my ordinary schedule, it was 3:00. When I walked in, Doug immediately asked me, "Have you heard about Tony?" I hadn't. He was in the hospital, he told me, the same hospital Mary's mother was now at. Johnny offered to drive me over. We left immediately. In what seemed like an instant, I found Tony lying on a hospital bed, on his side to avoid putting pressure on the back of his head, with his head elevated. A brown crease of dried blood stained the pillow where he had slept the night before. His mother, Jackie, his father (surprisingly), his Aunt Sharon and Sharon's two young children were all there as well. Jackie seemed calm, though I had heard she became hysterical the night before, her worst though ever-present fears, I imagined, made real. She said, "Tony, Greg's here" as I entered the room. Tony did not look up—I realized then that he couldn't—and said, "What's up, G," which was what he always said to me, and extended his hand weakly. But his speech was very, and untypically, slurred and slow. His mom said it was because of the medicine. But at this point, neurological damage was not ruled out and the implications were terrifying. We chatted for a few minutes (his mother was trying to let him rest). None of the boys who attacked him had been arrested, though there were warrants out for all of them. I couldn't believe how much damage one swing from a baseball bat could do.

Tony's grandfather drove him home later that week. I visited him soon after, finding him surrounded by his mom, his brothers, his sister, as well as several aunts, uncles, cousins, and friends. The room was dark and Tony wore sunglasses even inside (any kind of brightness hurt his eyes). He could not move from his sofa. His glasses had been broken in the assault and he could only listen to the television. A few friends had brought videos. I brought him my copy of *Goodfellas*, knowing that he liked gangster films. He had seen them all before and just sat, in the dark, his head down, listening to the dialogue, again and again. I asked Tony what his plans were. He felt better but said he woke up crying every morning at 5:00 a.m. and had constant headaches. He had to quit his job at a local fast food restaurant, and also stopped going to school. Though he enjoyed the alternative school he now attended, including the freedom it gave him to set his own schedule, his plans on graduating and becoming a teacher seemed to be on hold now. This situation was painful for another reason as well. Tony had been trying to "turn his life around" for a while and wanted to be a good role model for his younger brother, Rick, whom he feared might be making the same mistakes he had. He set up incentive programs for Rick's grades and also tried to keep track of his friends. He wanted to be the father figure neither of them ever had, though this incident, with its overtones of gang life and conflict, seemed to put that kind of authority in doubt.

That evening, Tony told me, they were having something for him at the club. It was a meeting for the community about violence. The meeting, organized by one of Tony's claimed "aunts," began at 7:30. Lots of people showed up—about 75—on very short notice. Several of Tony's cousins were there. So were many parents. Rufus came as well. Doug spoke first and said that he was from the Junior Egyptian Lodge, an organization that is supposed to build character among young men. He said he wanted to meet once a month with parents and target problems with teens, in hopes of avoiding events such as these. Doug spoke about the importance of "listening to elders" and how this ethic had been lost. He went on, saying that parents used to have the authority to "punish other people's kids" but they don't anymore—the implied sense of community and control, now gone. People applauded loudly. An elderly lady then said that the Department of Children and Family Services (DCFS) stops you from chastising other people's children now. She said that kids feel lost and stressed, and that you need to listen to and encourage them. Doug agreed, stressing that kids can always come to him with their problems.

Rufus was the first teen to speak up. He said that sometimes younger people had questions and "wanted someone with authority who would give us answers." Echoing the discussion of Chapter 4, the importance of balancing authority and care, he said, "But the love needs to be there, too." A teen girl then spoke up, agreeing, saying that younger kids often feel like they "have no mentors." Rufus then said that older people need to listen and also show guidance. Conceding somewhat, he talked about how some young people have a "chip on their shoulder" about dealing with older people. But they should not be afraid to discuss issues openly. Clearly, there was mistrust on both sides of the generational divide—there was work to be done in repairing these fissures. We ended by getting in a circle, holding hands, and praying.

Since late 1998, Tony and Rufus's lives have been, in large measure, about how they navigate their way between multiple institutions, this space of "the in-between"—the healthcare system, public assistance, the court system, school, and so on. They did not traverse these institutions in predictable ways. Their lives were propelled by here-and-now immediacies, by various and unpredictable social vicissitudes. Indeed, my efforts to write a simple story about these teens and this club were derailed by events put in motion that fall, events that would continue to spin out in terrible ways over the next several weeks and months.

After several weeks of incapacitation, Tony managed to take a job at a supermarket. After he was attacked, Tony had to give his clothes to the police as evidence and wanted to buy a new outfit. His glasses had also been broken in the fight and he needed a new pair. Seemingly small losses, they necessitated his getting back in the swing of things, getting a job. I drove him to his first night on the job. He was, he told me, a little afraid of being in public, of "the boys he was into it with" coming after him. Having an older white person around was good protection. I stopped by several times to check up on him over the next few days, to see how he was doing, if he needed a ride back. One evening, I ran into another one of the club members, a teenage girl, who told me that Tony had left the job. He had been attacked by Chris's brother and was now down South.

I got a collect call from Tony a few days later. He was staying at his grandmother's house. Tony told me he was planning on going into Job Corps in a few days—a vocational program for low-income youth that teaches job skills as well as life skills. It was good to leave town, he said, to "get away from it all." Johnny suggested it, saying that he should simply "go away" as soon as possible. Tony liked Job Corps. Young people lived together in a dormitory and got three meals a day, as well as basic dental and medical care. One was also able to earn a GED, which became a priority. Always hard-working, Tony had first gotten into brick laying, but soon after moved to cooking. He always excelled at these jobs, learning what he had to know much faster than expected. Tony had, recall, lots of experience working in fast-food restaurants like McDonald's, Burger King, and Wendy's. He was also well liked by most of the teachers there, though he also had the occasional clash of wills, as he did with several authority figures in his life. Tony told me that one of the older counselors was a Lodge member and he was talking to him about starting a Junior Egyptian Lodge program there. Tony tried orchestrating activities here— much like he did at the club—including dances, trips, and talent shows. Soon, he told me, he and a bunch of other people had formed what he called a "New Jack Clique." He also, he told me, informally counseled young people there.

I saw much more of Rufus, of course, during this period. While Tony navigated his way through Job Corps, Rufus was caring for his mother. With Mary now at home, Rufus had to devote himself fully to her care. He had to take care of the house, to clean, to cook, to help pay the bills, to "prepare her needle," to help figure out an endless set of health-care forms. As always, it was the two of them, together. Mary was fiercely independent, though of course had enormous needs. At one point, she requested some help in the home from social services. The questionnaire they sent her, she said, made her "feel helpless." "Can you do your hair?" "Can you do the things you used to do?" it asked. "I need the aide," she said, "but don't want to seem helpless." She never mailed the form in. Rufus continued to care for her, their lives often made sustainable by small acts of kindness towards each other. I recall going to Best Buy with Rufus to shop for a CD one evening. He wanted the new album by R-Kelly, a popular R&B artist. However, he bought an album by the group LeVert instead. Both he and his mother, he said, would enjoy that one. They spent almost all their time together in the house.

That February, as I said earlier, Mary entered the hospital for the last time. Rufus called me and asked me to drive them over. Mary was tired. Upset, she said she was "tired of being tired." Rufus put her coat over her shoulders and said, "Stop all that crying." We went to the bank to cash the check that she had from the Department of Social Services. Rufus asked her for a dollar. Handing over the money, she said, "What would you do if I wasn't here?" He said, "Ask Greg." Later that afternoon, she said, "What are we going to do without Greg?" Both knew I was interviewing for academic jobs and would soon be leaving town.

It was a trying time. Rufus always had to act as the man, always had to be the one who interfaced with the hospital staff. While he endeared himself to many of the nurses, the doctors were often another story. When Mary was admitted, the doctor had to begin an IV to start draining the fluids. The doctor had a hard time finding a vein. Mary was in pain, crying. Rufus protested. "If you're going to stay here," the doctor snapped, "you're going to need to let me do my job!" Trying to lighten the mood, I imagined, he then said to one of the nurses, "I bet you a Coke I can get it in one shot." Rufus was devastated. "I wanted to kick his ass," he told me, "or cuss him out—but my vocabulary's not so good."

With Mary in the hospital now, Rufus had to take over all the household responsibilities. The night after Mary was admitted, he called and left a message on my machine, asking if I would be willing to come meet him in the waiting room. I got the message late and by the time I got there, he had left to go home. I drove over to his place. It was about 10:30 p.m. A few of the kids from the neighborhood were there. Rufus was counting pennies and had a few $2 bills out (which I assume had been saved as collectibles). He said he didn't like taking his mom's money but was hungry. It was getting late, but I said I would pick them up some pizzas, which I did. Later in the evening, close to midnight, Rufus and I sat on the porch with one of his friends, Lewis. Lewis was talking about his grandmother, how she got diabetes because of eating fatty foods. He was trying to comfort Rufus, to find some common ground. The mood was somber. It was late. From here on out, he would be alone in the house, alone until he was eventually evicted for having too many teenagers hanging around, all hours of the night.

A month later, the Department of Children and Family Services became involved. Rufus, though a man in so many ways, was 3 months shy of 18. He was technically still a minor. Johnny first told me how serious the situation was; he said, "a social worker is now involved." Johnny said that Rufus could not sustain the situation by himself and needed a lot of help. He said he was impressed by how his school was handling it, that they contacted him often. Johnny said that he "broke it down" for Rufus, laying out the situation and his options. He told Rufus to make sure that his house was clean and he had lots of food in the refrigerator. He said not to have his friends hanging out and drinking. He then said, "I admire Rufus more than anyone else in the world! I don't know how he does it! . . . I hope DCFS lets him go but if they don't I'll adopt him until he's eighteen." No longer unit director at the club, Johnny still played a critical role in his life. Johnny, it seemed, considered Rufus his son already.

DCFS came by soon after to look at the living conditions. Rufus spent the day cleaning up the house. I bought him food for his refrigerator. He told me that he was lucky he had so much family around him—including me. He told me his mom said, "I can't decide if Greg is a brother or a son." We visited his mom every few days or so, in the hospital and also in the nursing home in which she soon began living, from the day she was admitted until I left 5 months later.

At one point, early in March, Rufus's relatives came up from the South, to perhaps convince him and his mom to come live with them. Johnny told me, haltingly, that it was probably a good idea. They were going to stay at Rufus's house. He did not have a shower curtain and wanted to get one for the visit. We drove over to K-Mart. Rufus was ambivalent about the idea of leaving. He missed his family. While he clearly needed help caring for his mom, he did not like the idea of leaving school and starting someplace new. Plus, the schools there were not as "advanced" as the schools in Hub City, a feeling that both he and Tony had expressed to me several times. As we shopped, mulling over his situation, he told me about his new girlfriend, Janice, who was also causing him some stress.

I had become fairly used to hearing about Rufus and Tony's relationships. Talk about who was "playing" whom, who was worth committing to and why, as noted, was commonplace. I had never seen either in this kind of real emotional pain, however. This seemed different. Janice came from an abusive home and was coming to cling closer and closer—in fact, too close—to him. Social services was involved, but she still wanted Rufus to come over almost every night and spend time with her. He tried to explain that he had to be with his mom but she, in dire trouble and only an adolescent herself, would not listen. She had also gotten wind of his potential plans to move and he had to assure her—falsely—that he had no intention of leaving. He then said Janice and his mom both cried around him a lot and tried to get him to cry as well. Both got mad when he didn't. "My crying days are over," he said as he continued to sift through shower curtains, comparing prices, preparing to make the house up for his guests.

Meanwhile, trouble was looming on the horizon for Tony. When Tony moved up to Job Corps, he asked me to send him a copy of the book *Nation of Lords*, about the Vice Lords written in the 1960s. I was hesitant. Though I knew it was a well-regarded autobiography, I knew that Job Corps was very strict about gang paraphernalia and might mistakenly consider it as such. He assured me this wasn't the case—it was just like a piece of history. Yet, my suspicions were soon confirmed. Under the pressure of close association with youth his own age, Tony was flirting with gang life again. He told me that he had gotten into some trouble over some photographs. He felt he needed to get away, if only temporarily.

Early in April, Tony returned from Job Corps for a visit. He had photographs, the ones I assumed he had gotten in trouble for. They were of young, shirtless men throwing up gang signs. One person had his fingers entwined into a five-point star. Another was throwing up the Hoover Deuce Crip sign. At first, I didn't recognize Tony. His eyes were stony. He was bent down, a Pirates hat cocked to the left. His fingers, quite plainly, cocked in the Vice Lords style. He was, he told me, "inactive" but still a Vice Lord. Still, he saw himself as a kind of mediator. He called me later that week after he retured and said that he was friends with someone in a rival gang. "He GD and I'm Vice Lord but we real cool . . . we have a 'thick and thin' clique." He also said that they had a formed a peace treaty. Though there were still a lot of fights, he said that he tried to "be a councilor" in such situations. Still there were other signs of trouble.

Ever the entrepreneur, Tony had begun buying cigarettes and selling them piecemeal. He would, he told me, sometimes extend credit. The staff called this "loan sharking." He called it making a living. Sure enough, he was eventually kicked out. The staff identified him as the head of the Vice Lords and Bloods alliance at the site. He was only, he reiterated to me and others, trying to orchestrate a truce between all the gang factions at the site. But he was kicked out nevertheless. He moved to Mississippi, then to Tennessee.

As April came to a close, throughout this all, Rufus was shackled with more and more responsibility. He had to care for the house and also visit his mom regularly, who was by this point at a local nursing home. Mary seemed to like the nursing home more than the hospital. The first time I visited her was to bring her antenna for her TV. Her hair, I saw, had been neatly braided. She told me one of the nurses had done it. The nursing home staff was almost exclusively black. Mary said she was glad to get out of the hospital, that she thought that the nurses there were rude to her. She said she overheard one of them saying one night, "We do too many things for her . . . she's gonna die anyway." She said she could not remember if she dreamed this or if she heard it—she was "out of it" most of the time. Later on, she said that "if they don't think that anyone is there to help you, they treat you bad." She said she always felt better when Rufus came by. Rufus and I went to see the movie *The Matrix* later that night. Rufus said he felt good because his mom gave him money for the movies like she used to when she had it. It brought back memories: "She said 'give me my purse'—it felt good!"

With Mary in the nursing home full-time, Rufus came increasingly to take care of himself, dealing constantly with the minor events that often came to rule the day. For example, Rufus got a toothache early that May. A seemingly small problem, it had been festering for some time. He had been treating it with Tylenol and then applying Ambesol directly to his tooth. In fact, he was applying close to a bottle of Ambesol a day before he began waking up, crying from the pain. Rufus finally called me and asked me to take him to the dentist. He also asked me to call his school, and tell him he would not be in. I did. Rufus had a hard time finding his medical card. We spent most of the morning looking through drawers and boxes. Finally, he found an old one. He got lucky. Less than a month from his 18th birthday and his graduation, he could still use public services. Once he turned 18 and left school, he was without any care whatsoever. We were late for the appointment. The woman, however, understood that he had a hard situation with his mother. As it turned out, he had serious problems—three teeth had very deep cavities and his wisdom teeth needed to be pulled. We scheduled another appointment and I took him to the hospital, where all these teeth would have to be pulled.

Mary was soon in dialysis. She was constantly shuttled between the nursing home (where she lived) and the hospital (where she often went in emergencies) and the dialysis center (for kidney treatments). By early June, she developed what was known as a resistant staph infection. Rufus didn't really know what this meant. I didn't either at the time. The first time I visited, Mary was in isolation at the hospital. One had to wear gloves and a mask to go into her room. Rufus felt that it was racist. The woman that she shared a room with, he said, was a "big-shot person who complained about her coughing." Mary often coughed quite violently; I had, of course, noticed this. He continued, "But we been around her when she cough. It don't mean nothing!" The sign on her door said that she was an "infected patient," that we needed to wear a mask and gloves and if we were to be within 3 feet of her. Rufus put his on right away. I followed his lead.

Mary was watching TV. We stayed and chatted for a while—Mary was feeling sick, but was happy we came, and was also happy that we were wearing the protective clothes. Still, she said that if she were really infectious, they would have quarantined her food. She knew this from working at a hospital several years ago. Rufus agreed. At one point, he took his mask off and said, "Anything she got, I'll get!" Of course, I was in a difficult situation. I did not yet know what this infection was— although according to Rufus, once you had it, you had it forever. Instinctively, however, I took off my mask as well. Mary protested, but to no avail. When we left, Rufus kissed her, though she tried to push him away. He said, "I'm doing something I'm not supposed to do."

I learned later that the protection was for her. These infections immunize you to a certain kind of antibiotics. They are often transmitted in hospitals, by constant use of needles. Interestingly, however, when Mary returned to the nursing home, the staff seemed little concerned with all this. While a sign on her door warned that she had this infection, that protective gear should be worn, they freely—and without protective gear—interacted with her, braiding her hair, helping her with her food, and so on. This was, to me, a complex and risky moment. The nurses seemed to be recognizing Mary's embodied humanity in tacit and powerful ways, just as they seemed to be putting her at risk for infection. It was a complex set of issues, overlaid by racial dynamics and histories. The nurses at the hospital were white, while the nurses at the nursing home were black. Rufus, as always, had to disentangle these issues, mostly on his own.

BECOMING MEN

That summer, the summer of 1999, I received my Ph.D. and left Hub City for Buffalo, New York. Rufus came to my graduation. He met my family for the first time. Along with my mother, father, sister, and aunt, he attended the ceremony and dinner afterwards. We all visited his mother in the nursing home that afternoon, as well: "I don't know what I'm gonna do without Greg!" she said.

The last time I saw Mary was on the Fourth of July. It was my last day in Hub City. We all celebrated the holiday at Tony's aunt's house. I planned on meeting Rufus the next day for breakfast at a diner, right before I left for the 14-hour trip. He paid for the meal. A month later, Tony called to tell me that Mary had died. He asked me, in tears, "Have you heard?" He told me that the funeral would be down South and promised to call me back with funeral information, which he soon did. Perhaps paradoxically, I got a clearer sense of things from Rufus, whom I called right away. Mary was taken to the hospital the night before, he told me, as she had had trouble breathing. Her breathing had seemed frighteningly labored to me before I left Hub City, so it was difficult to imagine just how much worse it had gotten. Rufus had already quit his job at a packing plant, the 4:00 a.m. to 1:00 p.m. shift, as he feared leaving his mom alone at night. As it was, he spent many sleepless nights hearing her heavy breathing in the next room. I had been encouraging when we spoke last. The doctors had let her return home which, I said, was a good sign, considering she had moved between the intensive care unit at the local hospital to the dialysis center to a nursing home for over 6 months. I was wrong, of course. I imagine, now, the doctors had let her return home to spend as much time as possible with her son.

There was no airport near the small town of Humbrick, so I landed in Johnson City, the larger town nearby. I rented a car when I landed, and drove down the highway, straight to the small town about which I had heard so much over the years. The contrasts in Humbrick were immediately striking. Placed along either side of the highway were—oddly, it seemed to me—palatial, residential mansions. Immediately off this main thoroughfare were smaller wooden shacks and trailers. Several of these shacks were, in fact, bars (or "cafes") and restaurants, which advertised with painted wooden signs. I saw only one small strip mall, with a McDonald's, a Dollar General, as well as drug, video, liquor, and shoe stores. People drove to nearby Johnson City, Tony told me, to do what he called "brand-name shopping."

Both Rufus and Tony had large families here, as I said, had grown up here together as small boys. Over those few days I was in Humbrick, I saw lots of the people I had just left in the city—several of Tony's cousins, as well as Tony's mother and sister. I also saw several of Rufus's aunts and uncles who I knew from their visits "up north." There was a lot of traffic back and forth between these sites, their notions of the "North" and "South" continually open to revision. Indeed, as Tony, Rufus, and I drove together through the streets of Humbrick the day before Mary's funeral—as we passed the school they both attended as youth—as we visited the plot of land Rufus's grandmother owned, where his uncle now had a trailer—as we passed by the abandoned house where Tony's grandmother had once run a semilegal "café"—they told me how much Humbrick had changed. Once so romanticized in their talk, they now told me "it just ain't the same."

The next day, Rufus eulogized his mother. Though they had come to rely on each other for everything, Rufus said, though he was now more alone than he ever would be, he felt very special. "If you never knew my mom," he said "I feel sorry for you." I sat in the back of the funeral home with Tony. He was silent. The funeral home was crowded, packed with all of Mary's siblings and their children, as well as Tony's family. That night, we went to Rufus's uncle's house. Someone turned on an Al Greene CD and the older folks danced. Someone put on hamburgers. At one point, one of Rufus's aunts asked Tony if he had a CD with that new song, "Back that Ass Up" by rapper Juvenile. She had heard it earlier that day on the radio. He had it. Soon the house reverberated with bass, as Juvenile rapped, "Back that ass up . . . back that ass up," a reference to dancing as well as sex. The older folks kept dancing. Everyone drank. Someone suggested playing "spades." A bunch of us got together and chose up teams. Of course, Rufus and Tony were partners.

The years since I left Hub City have been ones of struggle, replete with new senses of possibility. After traveling between the South and Hub City several times, Tony reentered Job Corps in 2000, after having been kicked out a year earlier. He told me, "I have to do this. I have to do this." He returned to studying food preparation, his previous concentration, and did very well, owing in large part to his experiences in fast food. However, he had a steadily growing problem with alcohol. Soon, he "came up dirty" on his urine test. He was asked to leave the program yet again. He moved back home to Hub City and soon started working as an assistant on a school bus, watching the kids. When he wasn't needed there anymore, he left the job, and began working as a busboy at a local restaurant. For a time, he lived with his girlfriend until he got into a fight with her dad and moved back to his mom's house. Keeping his little brother out of trouble didn't work out as he expected. His brother, Rick, was getting deeper and deeper into trouble and eventually had to go to juvenile jail for violating probation. He was sentenced to 180 days.

Tony continued to move in and out of trouble, as well. One night he and his friends were hanging out, drinking. The police rolled up on them and told them to move. He told the cop, "I ain't gotta move!" An argument ensued. Tony was charged with aggravated battery for assaulting a police officer. He faced 2–4 years in prison. His lawyer wanted him to plead out. He refused and said he wanted to go to court, to get another lawyer. Soon, I found out, the charge was reduced. Apparently, he wasn't accused of hitting the officer, but walking within the offer's immediate radius, "getting in his face" and putting his chest against the cop's finger, which was pointed at him. He admitted being drunk. He admitted yelling at the cop. He eventually pleaded guilty to the last part of the charge. He agreed to 10 days in the county jail and a year's probation. He would have happily taken more prison time for less probation, but this was not an option.

Tony seemed blasé about the prospect of going to county jail— "baby prison" as he called it. He knew people there. Indeed, many of his cousins "except Rufus" were or had been there. In fact, his "celly" or cell mate would turn out to be his uncle on his dad's side. A few weeks after the arrest, before he went to jail, he was admitted to the hospital for throwing up blood repeatedly. Apparently, he was developing a very serious pancreas problem due to his drinking. The revelation came as a surprise to me, though he had told me a few months earlier that he was going to celebrate his birthday by waking up and drinking hard liquor all day. After the incident, however, he told me he drastically cut down his drinking. He developed another stomach problem a few months later, but could not afford full care. He got some medicine from the doctor once, but did not go in for the follow-up. He couldn't afford it.

More and more, after he got out of jail and was on probation, Tony spent time at home. He feared going to back and needed to stay off the streets. This meant more and more isolation. He stopped seeing Rufus as regularly as he had, who now lived across town. His struggle, now more than ever, was to be a role model for his brother and others—an ideal that would increasingly motivate him.

TONY AND RUFUS'S REFLECTIONS ON
THE PAST, PRESENT, AND FUTURE

Rufus and Tony visited me several times since I moved to Buffalo. On these visits, we drove to Niagara Falls and Toronto, saw movies, watched videos, ate out, and talked. On one of these occasions, I suggested we talk about this book project, which I had been thinking about for a while. I suggested that we reflect on the last few years, what they had been through, what it meant to "grow up," to "be a man." After returning from a day in Toronto, we sat down and chatted in my living room, tape recorder running.

Rufus's life, of course, has been something of a struggle. When we talked, he was working as a janitor and also going to a local community college. He lived for a time with a group of friends, all splitting the bills. He told me one day that high school is about "what you are." College is about "what you're going to be." While he didn't do as well as he had hoped, he was "loving it all the way around." He told me that he had to take some remedial courses when he first got there:

First semester was good. I enjoyed it [but] I was a little bit below college courses. . . . I still have 099 English and 099 SSC [Study Skills Class], which is helping me with study skills. Your reading,

things like that . . . but I aced all that. That proves to me that I
shouldn't have been in there. But again, I was irritated by the
questions asked when I took that session. . . . I ain't so good with
English and all that stuff so I just got irritated and I just start
clicking, just went through it just to get it done. So, I just have to
get out of that habit, of not doing things I'm not interested in.

Second semester was more difficult:

Second semester . . . I went downhill then. Just jacking off. I
passed 099 English, SSC, and math barely. . . . But science initially was my major. Teaching. Education is what I have a passion
for. And I was gonna do a biology major, with a minor in mathe-
matics. That didn't work out, I shoulda did better in that. But I
realized that's too much information for me to be retaining. With
biology, you have to know a lot of things. And I tend to drift off
to other areas when it comes to explaining biology. Math is just
straightforward and simple—a lot of theories and formulas. Some
things I can come up with, like basically short cuts. . . . I learned
the hard way that math is what I really need to be taking care of.
So it kind of crushed me to go down in math. I didn't do so good
second semester. My grade point average dropped. I had a 3.0
first semester and then second semester, I got a 1.9.

I asked him if his dip in grades had anything to do with his grueling work
schedule. He said no, that he was actually doing the best when he worked
the longest hours. He said:

I was working at [a local middle school], like two months and a
half straight. Three months, which is I guess half the semester.
. . . I worked every day. That was tough. I worked from three to
eleven and my classes was from nine to one. By the bus systems
you only really get a good hour to study. Then I take off and go to
work, 'cause I had to be in work at three. I was working nine-
hour days. . . . I had to take care of 28 rooms. Which is a lot. I
think it's like, it may be 42 rooms in the school building, that's
classrooms. Then I had to do the gym, then there's the gym,

library, and the offices. . . . Just school, work, home, get some
rest, then do the same thing the next morning. And on the week-
ends, I didn't really go out. Second semester was when I refused
to work like that and I had a lot of time on my hands.

Moving in with four friends, he had increasingly to handle a limited
budget: "You can find a four-hundred-dollar two-bedroom and split it
with somebody, true, but you gotta realize, you splitting everything two
ways. This way, I'm splitting everything four ways. Means utilities,
phone, cable, which we don't have right now, 'cause that ain't no necessity."

Material pressures, thus, bore down on Rufus as he struggled his
way towards adulthood. While he was forced—largely unwillingly, he
stressed—to occupy adult roles early on, he felt conflicted. He saw himself as an unfinished project in this regard:

I think I have a long way to becoming a man. 'Cause there's a lot
of issues I have to work out. I mean, I got manly ways. I got the
structure of a man, physically. But mentally, I ain't got the
thought of a man. See what I'm saying? I ain't quite accomplished that. I don't know quite what it is I'm lacking, but you
can feel [it] and you'll know personally when you become a man.

While he discussed these issues with older folks like Johnny, he told
me, he also looked to his friends: "We question ourselves. This is between
the ages of eighteen and twenty-one. We question ourselves every day,
my circle of friends. Lot of people say, 'Oh, they ain't doing nothing but
drinking and smoking weed.' But we question ourselves." For example,
we see Rufus ask below what he is "supposed" to do "as a man" in a context where traditional gender roles have been undercut by material realities. Rufus considers here his future roles and responsibilities, the hypo-
thetical possibility of being a father and what this means:

[Say] I got this baby on the way. What am I supposed to do? How
am I supposed to take care of them? Am I supposed to go out and
buy diapers and food. . . . Am I supposed to make her be a
woman? Cook, clean? . . . Take care of my cleaning? Or should I

tell her . . . we do it together? And try to teach? How am I going
to teach my boy to be a man? How am I gonna help? . . . I mean,
we question ourselves.

We see him question here his material circumstances ("How am I supposed to take care of them?"), as he considers dominant and oppressive
gender expectations ("Am I supposed to make her be a woman? Cook,
clean?"), as well as more egalitarian relationships ("Or should I tell her .
. . we do it together?"). Many of these concerns, as he noted, were worked
through with friends—including of course, Tony. "Because," he said, "I
look up to Tony for certain things."

Tony said several times that he hoped to be a teacher, to help others
learn from his mistakes. While he was now working in food service, he
was still planning on getting his GED. But being a "teacher," I think,
implied something broader. For example, it meant trying to show people
how to "hustle"—to survive by any means—but to do it legally.

> I plan on going to school to be teacher. Help kids that's coming
> up the path that I went, up in the juvenile courts system to the
> adult court system, to where I'm at now. I know kids nowadays,
> like my little brother's age, fifteen, I know kids that's eleven or
> twelve, out there trying to sell drugs and everything. My goal is
> to stop it. 'Cause I been through it all. I been through it.

Tony seemed to know how young people fall into this kind of lifestyle—
the desire for money; the desire for recognition and respect; the desire to
make a mark in a world indifferent to your well-being. When I asked what
he might do to stop it all, he said,

> Tell them, basically show them where it leads to. Show them that
> you can still make quick money and hustle, but you can do it
> legally. You know? Like cutting grass, shoveling snow, raking
> leaves, that's what we used to do, right? Back in the day when we
> was young, make quick hustle. Selling drugs when we was young
> wasn't no big thing. Now most kids nowadays, they tend to
> wanna be known. They wanna be known by everybody and they
> feel selling drugs is the only way they can be known. No, man,
> you can be known by positive people instead of negative people.

Of course, his own younger brother was at the forefront of his mind. Tony understood the pressures facing him, the pressures of survival, and he understood their attendant dangers:

> Don't come to me asking for money all the time. . . . Get out
> there and hustle you some money up. You say you wanna job, but
> won't nobody hire you 'cause you ain't got no permit. So get out
> there do something where you won't need no work permit. Cut
> some grass, [in his brother's voice] "Well I aint got a lawn
> mower." Well, you go borrow a lawn mower, from someone who
> will let you use their lawn mower. You know? Man, rake leaves.
> "I ain't got no rake." Man if you start your own business, I can
> invest some money in you. But when you talk about things like,
> "I don't care, I'm gonna steal some bikes, or I'm gonna do this."
> Man I can't invest in that. 'Cause it's illegal. It's not helping you.
> You ain't learn nothing but the life of crime. I lived it. Your father
> lived it.

Tony was also, of course, conflicted around his own roles and responsibilities in this regard. While Tony always had to act as a father figure to Rick, he himself had succumbed to the pressures of the street over and over, even as he tried to extricate himself from it. It was a process, a struggle. No matter how many times he tried to turn away from the street, the pressure to fall into his old ways could overtake him. Sometimes events themselves overtook him, as they did when he was attacked at the park. Sometimes, he told me, he just said, "Fuck it!"

> Rick used to always say, "You stupid. You always getting in trou-
> ble with the police, you always going to jail for something. I ain't
> gonna never be like you." And then I turn around, he kinda make
> me feel guilty. . . . 'Cause as him being younger, six years
> younger than me, I wasn't holding up that big brother role. . . .
> 'Cause he don't have no father. And you know, basically, I was
> the man of the house at all times, you know, I was the man of the
> house since the age of nine. . . . And basically, I ain't know much
> about being a man of the house. But hey, I was there, I took care
> of, when I had money and they needed something, I would
> always give it to them. But I was always also living a bogus

lifestyle. I wasn't caring really, had an attitude problem, which was my number one problem was, my temper. . . . Suffered a lot of trouble, went to jail.

Like many role models, Tony was honest about his life, his successes and failures. As Rufus said, Tony always had good intentions, even when he didn't live up to them, even when he said, "Fuck it!" He tried always to speak from a caring space, a space of experience. Rufus said,

That's what's amazing about Tony. And that's why I love him. 'Cause it goes beyond, it's his talent and his gift to give, goes beyond just the community of Hub City. You know what I'm saying? Wherever he touch down and when he gets involved in people's lives in a positive sense. He explains his experiences, but at the same time, they explaining their experiences, he helps through observation, to help them mold themselves, let them know what they did wrong, other route they could have went about it, and how they shouldn't really dwell on it. Basically give them good advice.

Again, this advice is rooted in experience, in caring commitment to those around him. It was not the empty advice of professionals. "It's just not bogus advice," he said. "Because you can get bogus advice from a psychiatrist. . . . Or a teacher. People that's in professional positions. But when you somebody whose either been through it. I should say credible. They [have] the credit to say, 'Well, I done that, been there.' But at the same time, Tony saying, 'Well, I really don't understand what happened.'" Rufus continued, "He goes to work, keeps a job for a long time, people love him, managers, the lowest man on the totem pole at the job is crazy about him. So it's unique. He's a very unique individual. The only thing I always, from my observing, being around him, is he has good intentions."

Tony's life, thus, has been marked by struggle. But in the final analysis he still saw himself and was seen by others as a success in all kinds of ways. This is key. As noted earlier, youth like Rufus and Tony don't operate on a normative middle-class model, where "success" is measured in predictable ways and outcomes. Success, in this context, means something very different. Tony said:

I made it to twenty-one. Never been to a prison, thank God. . . . I don't count county as prison. That's just baby jail. I never got no kids. Twenty-one with no kids. And I'm not dead. So therefore I'm proud of myself. . . . 'Cause I'm not a statistic. I been in the judicial system. But I've never been to an adult prison. So I'm not in their statistics about that. Which, like I say, makes me proud of myself. I mean, I ain't to where I want to be. I know I could have been better to what I am.

Tony saw himself as a success, if an unfinished project.

THE RISKS AND REWARDS OF MEETING YOUNG PEOPLE IN THE IN-BETWEEN: FINAL THOUGHTS

In writing *Friendship, Cliques, and Gangs: Young Black Men Coming of Age in Urban America*, I have tried to tell a success story about urban youth, though perhaps an unpredictable or unusual one. I have spent much of this book highlighting the work these youth did moving from adolescence to adulthood, their friendships, their work at the club, their relationships with those older. I have also highlighted the dangers they faced and worked to avoid. I am hopeful but sober about their lives. I am aware that poverty makes Rufus and Tony both almost unimaginably vulnerable to any contingency life throws their way. I am aware that the emerging socioeconomic landscape will only make their lives much harder—as if they weren't hard enough already. I am aware that the lure of self-destructive dispositions and behaviors—alcoholism, violence, misogyny, despair, among them—looms ever-present.

It is impossible, given this context, to offer a simple set of conclusive prescriptions about what we as educators "need to do" today. Recall Rufus's comment earlier, about how one can get "bogus advice" from professionals, from teachers and psychiatrists. Sadly, they both speak from experience here. Recall, in contrast, his comments about Tony, about his willingness to talk openly about his own successes and mistakes, to admit when he couldn't really tell the difference between the two. Both these youth modeled a kind of disposition towards each other and towards me that I found immensely instructive, that seemed more important and profound than any specific policy intervention I might forward.

I won't end this book, therefore, by invoking some new "vanguard" movement or theory for urban education today. If nothing else, this work forced me, again and again, to try to understand processes that seemed largely beyond my control, a reality that constantly outstripped my predictive powers. As I hope I've made clear, this necessitated giving up my own certainties as a researcher, and entering into more human and caring kinds of relationships with these youth. Rearticulating these relationships forced me to ask different kinds of questions, to see in more complex and situated ways the array of issues and tensions young people were enmeshed in as they made the transition from adolescence to adulthood.

This meant, in part, decentering my own assumptions about education today. Education, I found, was an emergent phenomenon for these youth, unfolding across numerous sites and settings with and in between multiple texts—all of which worked with each other in complex ways, difficult to predict a priori. Schools, I found, were only one part of this complex nexus—and a perhaps minor one at that. Most of the work most relevant in their lives took place in the cracks and crevices between such official organizations, in places discussed throughout, such as the community center.

If we are to meet young people on this fraught and unpredictable terrain, I argue, we must take as open and expansive a disposition towards educational research and practice as possible. This book, I hope, is one example of what kind of work can emerge from such a disposition. More such work might lead us to more contextualized approaches to young people's lives today, approaches that look beyond normative models of development and the notions of "success" that often gird them. At best, such work might allow us to begin to "remap" pedagogical possibilities with young people today—possibilities for a pedagogy that takes place in the "in between," in the context of profoundly relational human and caring encounters. Indeed, it is the "in-between"—the moving back and forth—that increasingly defined these young people's lives. It is the "in-between" that came to define my "research" agenda. It is the "in-between," finally, where we must begin to rearticulate a relationship with urban youth.

APPENDIX

Qualitative Inquiry and the Complexities of Researcher–Researched Relations: A Methodological Appendix

As Lois Weis and Michelle Fine argue, "speed bumps" are unexpected moments in the research process when fieldworkers must slow down and reflect upon the practices and politics of qualitative inquiry. As should be evident by now, this book documented many such "speed bumps," contingencies that forced me to reflect on my own research goals as well as my relationship with and responsibility to the community center (in general) and these two young people (in particular). Time and again, my efforts at reciprocity forced me to rearticulate my relationship with the participants in this project, and also forced me to rearticulate my research agenda.

These tensions and contingencies speak broadly to the demands of qualitative research today, including newly acknowledged complexities around researcher-researched relations. Again, Weis and Fine prove helpful here. As Fine (1994) notes, fieldworkers today must "work the hyphen" in their different and overlapping identity positions (e.g., participant-observer, insider-outsider, self-other), always acknowledging the identities they inhabit, including what they allow and what they deny. According to Fine, researchers must actively work against "othering" in fieldwork, objectively creating neatly bounded subjects on which to report, while they must also resist self-reflexivity or navel gazing, the danger of looking inward as a way to avoid the ethical responsibility of acting in the world. Fine challenges us to avoid what Donna Haraway calls the "god-tricks" of "relativism" and "totalization." As Haraway (1991) writes, "Relativism is the perfect twin of totalization in the ideologies of objectivity; both deny the stakes in location, embodiment, and partial perspective" (p. 191). "Location, embodiment, and partial perspective" are critical to the project of ethnographic fieldwork, according to Fine.

More recently, Fine and Weis (1998) have extended these concerns to explicitly address the complexities of political activism and policy making. They argue in *The Unknown City*, that we must try to "meld *writing about* and *working with*" politically invested actors in more compelling and constitutive ways (p. 277, emphasis in original). Ultimately, they call us to "think through the power, obligations, and responsibilities of social research" on multiple levels, accounting for multiple social contexts and concerns (Fine, Weis, Weseen, & Wong, 2000, p. 108). In the end, self-reflexivity means increasing kinds of responsibility for such questions in a social context difficult to prefigure a priori. They sum up, "Our obligation is to come clean 'at the hyphen,' meaning that we interrogate in our writings who we are as we coproduce the narratives we presume to 'collect.' . . . As part of this discussion, we want, here, to try to explain how we, *as researchers*, work *with* communities to capture and build upon community and social movements" (Fine & Weis, 1998, pp. 277–278, emphasis in original). This means expanding the range of identities we inhabit as researchers, fieldworkers, and authors, to include political activism and policy making, identities that do not always map easily onto each other.

I have documented throughout my shifting position at the community center and in the lives of these young men. I have tried to situate my own changing location, while keeping the focus on these two teens. All this makes it difficult, however, to simply extract some exportable "method" here that would allow someone to "replicate" this study. It was simply too personal, too idiosyncratic an endeavor. At best, what I tried to offer here is a narrative that highlights this process, in all its complexity. More such stories, I believe, are critical: "Stories that lie beneath the surface of the final product, stories that need to come out and be thought through if we are to engage [qualitative inquiry] in a meaningful fashion" (Weis & Fine, 2000, p. 2).

Telling one such story, here, necessitates a broader discussion about what enabled this project to unfold as it did. To begin with, it means acknowledging that I was a single, childless man in my mid- to late 20s while I did this work. Moreover, I had secure university funding which allowed me to support myself (though barely) and didn't demand very much work. I didn't have very many personal responsibilities to crowd my life. My time was my own. All this allowed me to think in different ways about what reciprocity to this site and to these youth might mean. All this allowed me to respond to moment-to-moment demands in very flexible ways.

I would like to chart, now, some of the roles I occupied at this club and in this community, how my identity evolved and with what effects, how I was able to enter these young people's lives how and when I did. I said at the beginning of this book that one story ended and another began in 1998. I would like to discuss, now, what allowed that transition to happen the way it did.

REFLECTIONS ON RESEARCHING, VOLUNTEERING, AND WORKING AT THE COMMUNITY CENTER

During the 1995–1996 school year, I began conducting focus groups on black vernacular culture and the reception practices of black youth at this community center. I grew up in New York City and was enmeshed in multiracial and -ethnic social networks from a young age. In particular, I was very self-conscious about my complex relationship to and with black popular culture (generally) and hip hop culture (specifically) from a young age (Dimitriadis & McCarthy, 2000). However, upon first entering this site, I was clearly drawn into my "whiteness" in very particular ways. Indeed, Johnny, the unit director, was initially distrustful of me and the tenor was one of mutual manipulation. During one of our very first meetings, he noted with some enthusiasm that we were going "to use each other." He said that my program would "give our kids certain concepts that they could use in school," noting that black children are often afraid to speak up around white people. He also noted, perhaps most importantly, that I would be feeding "his kids" as well. I had agreed to bring pizza to every meeting, an important part of our deal.

During this initial period, I was treated like any other person conducting a project or acting as a volunteer. I had no authority at the club and my relationship to its members was mediated by the authority of the staff, including Johnny and the education director, Bill. I certainly was not in a position to meet out discipline or punishment, nor did I want to. I found this identity useful in lots of ways. Specifically, I began the long task of acquiring participants for my research project and collecting empirical material for my research on young people and popular culture—my main concerns.

In early 1997, I began volunteering at this site. It would be difficult to reconstruct my motivations for offering my services in any kind of complete way. On one level, I found myself reaching a kind of saturation with these focus groups, as I did not have the local, contextual knowledge of these young people's lives that would allow me to connect these texts to their lives in more particular kinds of ways. This kind of context, linked to a deeper understanding of the site and community, was missing. I decided to spend more time at the club, "hanging out," but without a more clearly defined role, this was awkward. In fact, I showed up one night and entered the TV room occupied by several teens, and sat down. When Johnny, the unit director, saw me, he asked, not kindly: "What are you doing here? It's not Monday [the night I conducted these sessions]."

Linked to these anxieties, I also began feeling that my status with older staff people like Johnny was changing—that I was somehow not fulfilling my part of the bargain and was, in some way, "using" the site and we were not "using" each other as originally planned. At one point, I asked Johnny if he was happy with the way my programming was going. He responded, "Well, you're getting what you need, put it like that." Thus, I became a volunteer that following year, in hopes of staying in everyone's good graces, in hopes of addressing power imbalances that could subvert my research plans.

If the tenor was one of mutual manipulation between myself and the club, I was more than fulfilling my part at this point in time, putting in over 15 hours of volunteer time a week doing a range of tasks. Though still an outsider, I was now something of a "golden boy." In short, I went from being a "bad" outsider to a "good" outsider very quickly and in perhaps inordinate ways. When I was wholly distrusted early on, now, it seemed, I was placed on something of a pedestal. My identity as a white researcher was both fetishized and marginalized, it seems, two sides of the same coin. During a staff training session, Bill singled me out to the rather large group as a volunteer "who helped out a lot," noting that "we really depend on Greg" to perform a number of important tasks. On another occasion, Johnny pulled me aside and told me, "You have been a great asset to this organization and I'll never forget it." He then called me a "jewel." However, I still had little real authority at the club and was not responsible for the club and its daily functioning.

This was, in retrospect, a very fruitful period. I was able to conduct these focus groups, though my increasing access to the club also allowed me to see key participants more regularity, allowing for a depth of familiarity that would greatly enrich my work. In particular, my ongoing presence allowed me to conduct more focused case study research, to complement the group dynamics I was limited to in focus groups. Regularly attending the club was critical for their success. Young people were typically very busy and typically unorganized and pulled in many different directions, making set appointments difficult if not impossible. My constant presence made such contact immeasurably easier. It was during this period that I began interviewing Rufus and Tony, both individually and at times together. Several of these interviews were used at various points throughout this book.

At the end of the spring of 1997, after several months of volunteering, I was offered a staff position. Bill suggested it, noting that I did so much during the year that I should be getting paid for it. I did not expect the offer, but felt obligated to take it, though I had—in retrospect, warranted—fears that my research agenda would be subverted or derailed. Demands were in fact put on me here in ways that inextricably changed the nature of my fieldwork, in ways that had very serious implications for the kind of research I was able to pursue. To echo the above discussion, working with people is not always simple and one cannot always dictate the agenda a priori. During this period as a staff member, my identity as a white person at this site was wrapped up in day-to-day questions, concerns, and demands. My "whiteness" was open to new kinds of possibilities and effectivities—though I also learned the limits to that rearticulation, the lines I would never and could never cross.

Specifically, I was hired to coordinate summer activities in the multipurpose room. Much of this story was recounted in Chapters 3 and 4—the importance of the community center, the importance of Johnny as a caring protective figure. I will not rehash this discussion here. Suffice to say, I witnessed a locally validated ethic of caring which allowed Johnny to act as a kind of extended family member—with all its attendant responsibilities—toward these young people. It was a protective, caring, and authoritarian role—a role, as I noted earlier, I found difficult to occupy.

Indeed, I did not always perform up to the standards of Johnny, which caused many problems. When I first started watching the multipurpose room, before Tony stated working with me, I found myself granting too much latitude or leeway to these young people. I found myself telling them to do whatever they wanted—and then when my weak, child-centered efforts failed, getting upset. When chaos ensued with these young people—young people on summer break—I often found myself raising my voice. Though Johnny was often quite stern with these young people, often deploying an extremely authoritarian style of discipline, he told me one day that yelling was not an appropriate way of dealing with children and I would have to show that I was fair with them. He said that control—and concurrently, respect—would come when the children saw me as a fair person. A good indicator, he noted, would be when the children came to me with their problems. They rarely did.

In counterdistinction, as noted earlier, Johnny was routinely enlisted by young people to solve all kinds of problems—from how to pay for college to how to get a job to how to deal with teachers to how to solve romantic problems. Above all else, these young people saw Johnny as fair. Even when they were in trouble at the club, young people always recognized and appreciated that they had the opportunity to tell their side of the story and get a fair hearing. The club, as opposed to school, was marked as unique in this regard. In fact, when I asked Johnny for tips on how to deal with young people in conflict, he told me to separate the two participants, get both sides of the story, see if there were any witnesses, speak to each separately, and then make a judgment based on all this evidence. He tried, above all else, to be as fair as possible.

Johnny could also be a fierce disciplinarian, however. After hearing both sides of the story from young people, he could be very strict and clear about who was in the right and who was in the wrong and had no problem expelling those in the wrong. However, this kind of seemingly authoritarian disciplining, I came to see, always seemed linked to keeping the club a safe environment. It was linked, as well, to an acute understanding of the risks and dangers these young people faced when they left the club—risks and dangers from others in the neighborhood as well as from broader society. As I came to see, the stakes are exceedingly high for these black youth, whose misbehavior is often criminalized with all the severity the state can muster. This is a deeply internalized, embodied kind of local knowledge for older and younger people here, one that informs everything from the deployment of language to physical comportment in different sociospatial contexts.

One example stands out. I routinely observed Johnny, Bill, and other senior staff members criminalize the misbehavior of youth, telling errant children that their actions and attitudes would "wind them up in prison" or that they "were going down the wrong path" to an early grave. At first, I saw this as a way in which oppression is internalized and reproduced through language practices. Yet, as I became immersed in the club and the lives of its members—as I saw the arbitrary and racist power of the juvenile criminal justice system—the caring and necessary dimensions to these practices became exceedingly pronounced. In some sense, one's "attitude" in front of the police, in front of judges, quite literally meant the difference between freedom and captivity. Being a competent disciplinarian was a skill I came to understand as complex and difficult, though extremely important, especially for ensuring the well-being of young people (on multiple levels) at this site.

However, it is critical to note that I was divorced from the lived reality that made such a position wholly tenable. Though I was a staff person, I could not engage young people as did Johnny. I was always still a "white guy" from outside the community no matter how close I grew to the young people or to this site. My whiteness effected clear and present borders and boundaries, ones I could not and would not traverse. Quite simply, no matter how long I spent at the site, no matter how close I got to these young people, a statement such as, "I can see it now, you're headed for jail" would have always deemed me—rightfully—a racist. I thus occupied a fraught and ever-negotiated terrain. New responsibilities and new meanings were attached to who I was as a white researcher all along the way. However, in no sense did my whiteness become less relevant over time.

My alignment with the club's authority was not always easy and had some serious repercussions for myself and my work. My responsibilities, from the point that I became staff onwards, went beyond simply my informants and my research but extended to the club, its other members, staff and volunteers, and the broader community. Often these investments worked directly against one another. With my relatively newfound responsibility for the site, I was less able to align myself with individual informants. A kind of uncritical trust was thus compromised. Yet I at least gestured towards new kinds of trust here, trust rooted in a ecologically validated ethic of caring.

It was at this point that my relationship with Rufus and Tony deepened. After our experiences working at the club together, I was positioned as an older, caring person who could be unconditionally relied upon for certain kinds of things. While I could never offer the kind of guidance that Johnny could—in the end, I was too disconnected from their lived realities—I could be there and was there in other kinds of ways. This did not mean meta-commentary on their lives. It meant the kind of mundane, everyday tasks recounted throughout this book—help with laundry and shopping, rides to Saturday morning football games, a drive back from an out-of-town college visit, rides to the hospital and dialysis center. That, quite simply, was my value in their lives. And it was the basis upon which our relationship deepened in, again, the ways described throughout.

FINAL THOUGHTS

There are, in closing, no safe spaces for ethnographers today. The notion of an objective and neutral qualitative inquiry has been called wholly into question, leaving researchers, to echo Mikhail Bakhtin (1993), no alibis for their effectivity in the field. What is left in the absence of foundational claims and clear splits between researchers and researched, is a profoundly uncertain terrain that asks us—demands us, really—to work with our participants to help make situations better than we found them. "The moral imperative of such work," Lincoln and Denzin (2000) argue, "cannot be ignored."

We thus face ever-present and unavoidable choices about our commitment to the people with whom we work—choices that have implications for all manner of ethnographic practice. The moment demands much from us. Having some guiding ethical beliefs can help. During the years of work discussed throughout, I embraced this community center (in general) and Rufus and Tony (in particular) in unwavering solidarity. This ethic of solidarity and commitment was rooted in a profound sense of care for the young people and staff members who attended this club and allowed me into their lives. In the end, those commitments alone helped me through the often painful and always rewarding years I spent with these young people. I hope others find my experiences helpful in thinking through their own personal and institutional commitments— their own ethics of solidarity, rooted in their own feelings of care.

I don't mean to pose this as a simple answer to a complex question, though. Taking such commitments seriously means always and ever facing complex sets of dangers—the danger of having others rearticulate your work and your life in unpredictable ways among them. Such are the now permanent dangers and risks—and joys and possibilities—of qualitative inquiry today.

References

Allan, G. (1998). Friendship, sociology, and social structure. *Journal of Social and Personal Relationships, 15*(5), 685–702.

Anderson, E. (1990). *Streetwise: Race, class, and change in an urban community.* Chicago: University of Chicago Press.

Anderson, E. (1999). *Code of the street: Decency, violence, and the moral life of the inner city.* Chicago: University of Chicago Press.

Bakhtin, M. M. (1993). *Towards a philosophy of the act* (V. Liapunov, Trans.). Austin: University of Texas Press.

Baldwin, J. (1955). *Notes of a native son.* Boston: Beacon Press.

Behar, R. (1996). *The vulnerable observer: Anthropology that breaks your heart.* Boston: Beacon Press.

Bing, L. (1992). *Do or die.* New York: HarperPerennial.

Burton, L., Obeidallah, D., & Allison, K. (1995). Social context and adolescence: Perspectives on development among inner-city African-American teens. In L. Crockett & A. Crouter (Eds.), *Pathways through adolescence: Individual development in relation to social contexts* (pp. 119–138). Mahwah, NJ: Lawrence Erlbaum Associates.

Burton, L., Obeidallah, D., & Allison, K. (1996). Ethnographic insights on social context and adolescent development among inner-city African-American teens. In R. Jessor, A. Colby, & R. Shweder (Eds.), *Ethnography and human development: Context and meaning in social inquiry* (pp. 395–418). Chicago: University of Chicago Press.

Cummings, S., & Monti, D. (Eds.) (1993). *Gangs: The origins and impact of contemporary youth gangs in the United States.* Albany: State University of New York Press.

Dawley, D. (1973). *A nation of lords: The autobiography of the Vice Lords.* New York: Doubleday.

Denzin, N., & Lincoln, Y. (2000). *Handbook of qualitative research* (2nd ed.). Thousand Oaks, CA: Sage.

Devine, J. (1995). *Maximum security: The culture of violence in inner-city schools.* Chicago: University of Chicago Press.

Dimitriadis, G. (2001a). *Performing identity/performing culture: Hip hop as text, pedagogy, and lived practice.* New York: Peter Lang.

Dimitriadis, G. (2001b). Coming clean at the hyphen: Ethics and dialogue at a local community center. *Qualitative Inquiry, 7*(5), 578–597.

Dimitriadis, G., & Carlson, D. (Eds.). (2003). *Promises to keep: Cultural studies, democratic education, and public life.* New York: Routledge Falmer Press.

Dimitriadis, G., & McCarthy, C. (2000). Stranger in the village: James Baldwin, popular culture, and the ties that bind. *Qualitative Inquiry, 6*(2), 171–187.

Dimitriadis, G., & McCarthy, C. (2001). *Reading and teaching the postcolonial: From Baldwin to Basquiat and beyond.* New York: Teachers College Press.

Dimitriadis, G., & Weis, L. (2001). Imagining possibilities with and for contemporary youth: (Re)writing and (Re)visioning education today. *Qualitative Research, 1*(2), 223–240.

Dryfoos, J. (1998). *Safe passage: Making it through adolescence in a risky society.* New York: Oxford University Press.

Dunier, M. (1992). *Slim's table: Race, respectability, and masculinity.* Chicago: University of Chicago Press.

Eckert, P. (1989). *Jocks and burnouts: Social categories and identity in the high school.* New York: Teachers College Press.

Fine, M. (1994). Working the hyphens: Reinventing self and other in qualitative research. In N. Denzin & Y. Lincoln (Eds.), *Handbook of qualitative research* (pp. 70–82). Thousand Oaks, CA: Sage.

Fine, M., & Weis, L. (1998). *The unknown city: Lives of poor and working-class young adults.* Boston: Beacon Press.

Fine, M., Weis, L., Centrie, C., & Roberts, R. (2000). Educating beyond the borders of schooling. *Anthropology & Education Quarterly, 31*(2), 131–151.

Fine, M., Weis, L., Wessen, S., & Wong, L. (2000). For whom? Qualitative research, representations, and social responsibilities. In N. Denzin & Y. Lincoln (Eds.), *Handbook of qualitative research* (2nd ed.) (pp. 107–131). Thousand Oaks, CA: Sage.

Gordon, A. (1997). *Ghostly matters: Haunting and the sociological imagination.* Minneapolis: University of Minnesota Press.

Haraway, D. (1991). *Simians, cyborgs, and women.* London: Routledge.

Hauser, S. (1991). *Adolescents and their families: Paths of ego development.* New York: Free Press.

Heath, S. B. (1996). Ruling places: Adaptation in development by inner-city youth. In R. Jessor, A. Colby, & R. Schweder (Eds.), *Ethnography and human development: Context and meaning in social inquiry* (pp. 225–251). Chicago: University of Chicago Press.

Heath, S. B., & McLaughlin, M. (Eds.). (1993). *Identity and inner-city youth: Beyond ethnicity and gender.* New York: Teachers College Press.

Heath, S. B., & McLaughlin, M. (1994). The best of both worlds: Connecting community schools and community youth organizations for all-day, all-year learning. *Educational Administration Quarterly, 30*(3), 278–300.

Jankowski, M. S. (1991). *Islands in the street: Gangs and American urban society.* Berkeley: University of California Press.

Klein, M. (1995). *The American street gang: Its nature, prevalence, and control.* Oxford, UK: Oxford University Press.

Kotlowitz, A. (1992). *There are no children here: The story of two boys growing up in the other America.* New York: Doubleday.

Lesko, N. (2001). *Act your age: A cultural construction of adolescence.* New York: Routledge.

Lincoln, Y., & Denzin, N. (2000). The seventh moment: Out of the past. In N. Denzin & Y. Lincoln (Eds.), *Handbook of qualitative research* (2nd ed.) (pp. 1047–1065). Thousand Oaks, CA: Sage.

Major, R., & Billson, M. (1992). *Cool pose: The dilemmas of black manhood in America.* New York: Touchstone Books.

McCarthy, C. (1998). *The uses of culture: Education and the limits of ethnic affiliation.* New York: Routledge.

McLaughlin, M., Irby, M., & Langman, J. (1994). *Urban sanctuaries: Neighborhood organizations in the lives and futures of inner-city youth.* San Francisco: Jossey-Bass.

McLoyd, V., & Steinberg, L. (Eds.). (1998). *Studying minority adolescents: Conceptual, methodological, and theoretical issues.* Mahwah, NJ: Lawrence Erlbaum Associates.

Perkins, U. (1987). *Explosion of Chicago's black street gangs: 1900 to the present.* Trenton, NJ: Third World Press.

Rosaldo, R. (1993). *Culture and truth: The remaking of social analysis.* Boston: Beacon Press.

Sale, R. (1971). *The Blackstone Rangers: A reporter's account of time spent with Blackstone Rangers in Chicago's South Side.* New York: Random House.

Shakur, S. (1998). *Monster : Autobiography of an L.A. gang member.* New York: Addison-Wesley.

Sidel, R. (1978). *Urban survival: The world of working-class women.* Nebraska: University of Nebraska Press.

Stack, C. (1974). *All our kin: Strategies for survival in a black community.* New York: HarperTorchbook.

Steinberg, L. (1996a). Commentary: On developmental pathways and social contexts in adolescence. In L. Crockett & A. Crouter (Eds.), *Pathways through adolescence: Individual development in relation to social contexts* (pp. 245–253). Mahwah, NJ: Lawrence Erlbaum Associates.

Steinberg, L. (1996b). *Beyond the classroom: Why school reform has failed and what parents need to do.* New York: Simon & Schuster.

Suskind, R. (1998). *A hope in the unseen: An American odyssey from the inner city to the Ivy League.* New York: Broadway Books.

Weis, L., & Fine, M. (Eds.). (2000). *Construction sites: Excavating race, class, and gender among urban youth.* New York: Teachers College Press.

Wilson, W. (1996). *When work disappears: The world of the new urban poor.* New York: Vintage.

Wyn, J., & White, R. (1997). *Rethinking youth.* Thousand Oaks, CA: Sage.

Index

About the Author

Greg Dimitriadis is Assistant Professor in the Department of Educational Leadership and Policy at the University at Buffalo, State University of New York. His work has appeared in several books as well as journals, including *Annals of the American Academy of Political and Social Science*; *Anthropology and Education Quarterly*; *Ariel: A Review of International English Literature*; *British Journal of Sociology of Education*; *Discourse: Studies in the Cultural Politics of Education*; *Educational Theory*; *Popular Music*; *Qualitative Inquiry*; *Text and Performance Quarterly*; and *Theory and Research in Social Education*.

Dimitriadis is the author of *Performing Identity/Performing Culture: Hip Hop as Text, Pedagogy, and Lived Practice* and co-author, with Cameron McCarthy, of *Reading and Teaching the Postcolonial: From Baldwin to Basquiat and Beyond* (Teachers College Press). He is co-editor, with Dennis Carlson, of *Promises to Keep: Cultural Studies, Democratic Education, and Public Life*. Dimitriadis's next book, *Qualitative Approaches to Language and Literacy Research* (co-authored with George Kamberelis) will be the first volume in a new series on language and literacy research published by Teachers College Press, in association with NCRLL.